I0165789

On the Trail of Grant and Lee

Frederick Trevor Hill

Contents

ON THE TRAIL OF
GRANT AND LEE

BY

Frederick Trevor Hill

To Howard Ogden Wood, Jr.

Forward

During the early years of the Civil War someone tauntingly asked Mr. Charles Francis Adams, the United States Minister to England, what he thought of the brilliant victories which the confederate armies were then gaining in the field. "I think they have been won by my fellow countrymen," was the quiet answer.

Almost half a century has passed since that reproof was uttered, but its full force is only just beginning to be understood. For nearly fifty years the story of the Civil War has been twisted to suit local pride or prejudice in various parts of the Union, with the result that much which passes for American history is not history at all, and whatever else it may be, it is certainly not American.

Assuredly, the day has now arrived when such historical "make-believes" should be discountenanced, both in the North and in the South. Americans of the present and the coming generations are entitled to take a common pride in whatever lent nobility to the fraternal strife of the sixties, and to gather equal inspiration from every achievement that reflected credit on American manhood during those years when the existence of the Union was at stake. Until this is rendered possible by the elimination of error and falsehood, the sacrifices of the Civil War will, to a large extent, have been endured in vain.

In some respects this result has already been realized. Lincoln is no longer a local hero. He is a national heritage. To distort or belittle the characters of other men who strove to the end that their land "might have a new birth of freedom," is to deprive the younger generations of part of their birthright. They are entitled to the facts from which to form a just estimate of the lives of all such men, regardless of uniforms.

It is in this spirit that the strangely interwoven trials of Grant and Lee are fol-

lowed in these pages. Both were Americans, and widely as they differed in opinions, tastes and sympathies, each exhibited qualities of mind and character which
should appeal to all their fellow countrymen and make them proud of the land that
gave them birth. Neither man, in his life, posed before the public as a hero, and
the writer has made no attempt to place either of them on a pedestal. Theirs is a
very human story, requiring neither color nor concealment, but illustrating a high
development of those traits that make for manhood and national greatness.

The writer hereby acknowledges his indebtedness to all those historians whose
scholarly research has made it possible to trace the careers of these two great commanders with confidence in the accuracy of the facts presented. Where equally
high authorities have differed he has been guided by those who, in his judgment,
have displayed the most scrupulous impartiality, and wherever possible he has
availed himself of official records and documents.

The generous service rendered by Mr. Samuel Palmer Griffin in testing the
vast record upon which these pages are based, his exhaustive research and scientific analysis of the facts, have given whatever of authority may be claimed for the
text, and of this the writer hereby makes grateful acknowledgment. To Mr. Arthur
Becher he is likewise indebted for his careful studies at West Point and elsewhere
which have resulted in illustrations conforming to history.

Frederick Trevor Hill.
New York, September, 1911.

Chapter I
Three Civil Wars

England was an uncomfortable place to live in during the reign of Charles the First. Almost from the moment that that ill-fated monarch ascended the throne he began quarreling with Parliament; and when he decided to dismiss its members and make himself the supreme ruler of the land, he practically forced his subjects into a revolution. Twelve feverish years followed--years of discontent, indignation and passion--which arrayed the Cavaliers, who supported the King, against the Roundheads, who upheld Parliament, and finally flung them at each other's throats to drench the soil of England with their blood.

Meanwhile, the gathering storm of civil war caused many a resident of the British Isles to seek peace and security across the seas, and among those who turned toward America were Mathew Grant and Richard Lee. It is not probable that either of these men had ever heard of the other, for they came from widely separated parts of the kingdom and were even more effectually divided by the walls of caste. There is no positive proof that Mathew Grant (whose people probably came from Scotland) was a Roundhead, but he was a man of humble origin who would naturally have favored the Parliamentary or popular party, while Richard Lee, whose ancestors had fought at Hastings and in the Crusades, is known to have been an ardent Cavalier, devoted to the King. But whether their opinions on politics differed or agreed, it was apparently the conflict between the King and Parliament that drove them from England. In any event they arrived in America at almost the same moment; Grant reaching Massachusetts in 1630, the year after King Charles dismissed his Parliament, and Lee visiting Virginia about this time to prepare for his permanent residence in the Dominion which began when actual hostilities opened in the mother land.

The trails of Grant and Lee, therefore, first approach each other from out of the smoke of a civil war. This is a strangely significant fact, but it might be regarded merely as a curious coincidence were it not for other and stranger events which seem to suggest that the hand of Fate was guiding the destinies of these two men.

Mathew Grant originally settled in Massachusetts but he soon moved to Connecticut, where he became clerk of the town of Windsor and official surveyor of the whole colony--a position which he held for many years. Meanwhile Richard Lee became the Colonial Secretary and a member of the King's Privy Council in Virginia, and thenceforward the name of his family is closely associated with the history of that colony.

Lee bore the title of colonel, but it was to statesmanship and not to military achievements that he and his early descendants owed their fame; while the family of Grant, the surveyor, sought glory at the cannon's mouth, two of its members fighting and dying for their country as officers in the French and Indian war of 1756. In that very year, however, a military genius was born to the Virginia family in the person of Harry Lee, whose brilliant cavalry exploits were to make him known to history as "Light Horse Harry." But before his great career began, the house of Grant was represented in the Revolution, for Captain Noah Grant of Connecticut drew his sword in defense of the colonies at the outbreak of hostilities, taking part in the battle of Bunker Hill; and from that time forward he and "Light Horse Harry" served in the Continental army under Washington until Cornwallis surrendered at Yorktown.

Here the trails of the two families, AGAIN DRAWN TOGETHER BY A CIVIL STRIFE, merge for an historic moment and then cross; that of the Grants turning toward the West, and that of the Lees keeping within the confines of Virginia.

It was in 1799 that Captain Noah Grant migrated to Ohio, and during the same year Henry Lee delivered the memorial address upon the death of Washington, coining the immortal phrase "first in war, first in peace and first in the hearts of his countrymen."

Ulysses Grant, the Commander of the Union forces in the Civil War, was the grandson of Captain Grant, who served with "Light Horse Harry" Lee during the Revolution; and Robert Lee, the Confederate General, was "Light Horse Harry's" son.

Thus, for the THIRD time in two and a half centuries, a civil conflict between men of the English-speaking race blazed the trails of Grant and Lee.

Chapter II
Washington and Lee

Wakefield," Westmoreland County, Virginia, was the birthplace of Washington, and at Stratford in the same county and state, only a few miles from Wakefield, Robert Edward Lee was born on January 19, 1807. Seventy-five years had intervened between those events but, except in the matter of population, Westmoreland County remained much the same as it had been during Washington's youth. Indians, it is true, no longer lurked in he surrounding forests or paddled the broad Potomac in their frail canoes, but the life had much of the same freedom and charm which had endeared it to Washington. All the streams and woods and haunts which he had known and loved were known and loved by Lee, not only for their own sake, but because they were associated with the memory of the great Commander-in-Chief who had been his father's dearest friend.

It would have been surprising, under such circumstances, if Washington had not been Lee's hero, but he was more than a hero to the boy. From his father's lips he had learned to know him, not merely as a famous personage of history, but as a man and a leader of men. Indeed, his influence and example were those of a living presence in the household of "Light Horse Harry;" and thus to young Lee he early became the ideal of manhood upon which, consciously or unconsciously, he molded his own character and life. But quite apart from this, the careers of these two great Virginians were astonishingly alike.

Washington's father had been married twice, and so had Lee's; each was a son of the second marriage, and each had a number of brothers and sisters. Washington lost his father when he was only eleven years old, and Lee was exactly the same age when his father died. Mrs. Washington had almost the entire care of her son during his early years, and Lee was under the sole guidance of his mother until he had almost grown to manhood. Washington repaid his mother's devotion by caring for her and her affairs with notable fidelity, and Lee's tenderness and consideration for his mother were such that she was accustomed to remark that he was both a son and a daughter to her.

Washington's ancestors were notable, if not distinguished, people in England; while Lee could trace his descent, through his father, to Lancelot Lee, who fought at the battle of Hastings, and through his mother to Robert the Bruce of Scotland. Neither man, however, prided himself in the least on his ancestry. Indeed, neither of them knew anything of his family history until his own achievements brought the facts to light.

Washington was a born and bred country boy and so was Lee. Both delighted in outdoor life, loving horses and animals of all kinds and each was noted for his skillful riding in a region which was famous for its horsemanship. There was, however, a vast difference between Washington's education and that of Lee. The Virginian schools were very rudimentary in Washington's day; but Lee attended two excellent institutions of learning, where he had every opportunity, and of this he availed himself, displaying much the same thoroughness that characterized Washington's work, and the same manly modesty about any success that he achieved.

By reason of his father's death and other circumstances Washington was burdened with responsibility long before he arrived at manhood, making him far more reserved and serious-minded than most school boys. This was precisely the case with Lee, for his father's death, the ill health of his mother and the care of younger children virtually made him the head of the family, so that he became unusually mature and self-contained at an early age. Neither boy, however, held aloof from the sports and pastimes of his schoolmates and both were regarded as quiet, manly fellows, with no nonsense about them, and with those qualities of leadership that made each in turn the great military leader of his age.

Never has history recorded a stranger similarity in the circumstances surrounding the youth of two famous men, but the facts which linked their careers in later years are even stranger still.

Chapter III
Lee at West Point

As his school days drew to a close, it became necessary for Lee to determine his future calling. But the choice of a career, often so perplexing to young men, presented no difficulty to "Light Horse Harry's" son. He had apparently always intended to become a soldier and no other thought had seemingly ever occurred to any member of his family. Appointments to the United States Military Academy were far more a matter of favor than they are to-day, and young Lee, accompanied by Mrs. Lewis (better known as Nellie Custis, the belle of Mount Vernon and Washington's favorite grandchild), sought the assistance of General Andrew Jackson. Rough "Old Hickory" was not the easiest sort of person to approach with a request of any kind and, doubtless, his young visitor had grave misgivings as to the manner in which his application would be received. But Jackson, the hero of the battle of New Orleans in the War of 1812, only needed to be told that his caller was "Light Horse Harry's" son to proffer assistance; and in his nineteenth year, the boy left home for the first time in his life to enroll himself as a cadet at West Point.

Very few young men enter that institution so well prepared for military life as was Lee, for he had been accustomed to responsibility and had thoroughly mastered the art of self-control many years before he stepped within its walls. He was neither a prig nor a "grind," but he regarded his cadetship as part of the life work which he had voluntarily chosen, and he had no inclination to let pleasure interfere with it. With his comrades he was companionable, entering into all their pastimes with zest and spirit, but he let it be understood, without much talk, that attention to duty was a principle with him and his serious purpose soon won respect.

Rigid discipline was then, as it is to-day, strictly enforced at West Point, and demerits were freely inflicted upon cadets for even the slightest infraction of the rules. Indeed, the regulations were so severe that it was almost impossible for a cadet to avoid making at least a few slips at some time during his career. But Lee accomplished the impossible, for not once throughout his entire four years did he incur even a single demerit--a record that still remains practically unique in the history of West Point. This and his good scholarship won him high rank; first, as cadet officer of his class, and finally, as adjutant of the whole battalion, the most coveted honor of the Academy, from which he graduated in 1829, standing second in a class of forty-six.

Men of the highest rating at West Point may choose whatever arm of the service they prefer, and Lee, selecting the Engineer Corps, was appointed a second lieutenant and assigned to fortification work at Hampton Roads, in his twenty-second year. The work there was not hard but it was dull. There was absolutely no opportunity to distinguish oneself in any way, and time hung heavy on most of the officers' hands. But Lee was in his native state and not far from his home, where he spent most of his spare time until his mother died. Camp and garrison life had very little charm for him, but he was socially inclined and, renewing his acquaintance with his boyhood friends, he was soon in demand at all the dances and country houses at which the young people of the neighborhood assembled.

Among the many homes that welcomed him at this time was that of Mr. George Washington Parke Custis (Washington's adopted grandson), whose beautiful estate known as "Arlington" lay within a short distance of Alexandria, where Lee had lived for many years. Here he had, during his school days, met the daughter of the house and, their boy-and-girl friendship culminating in an engagement shortly after his return from West Point, he and Mary Custis were married in his twenty-fifth year. Lee thus became related by marriage to Washington, and another link was formed in the strange chain of circumstances which unite their careers.

A more ideal marriage than that of these two young people cannot be imagined. Simple in their tastes and of home-loving dispositions, they would have been well content to settle down quietly to country life in their beloved Virginia, surrounded by their family and friends. But the duties of an army officer did not admit of this, and after a few years' service as assistant to the chief engineer of the army in Washington, Lee was ordered to take charge of the improvements of the Mississippi River at St. Louis, where, in the face of violent opposition from the inhabitants, he performed such valuable service that in 1839 he was offered the position of instructor at West Point. This, however, he declined, and in 1842 he was entrusted with the task of improving the defenses of New York harbor and moved with his family to Fort Hamilton, where he remained for several years. Meanwhile, he had been successively promoted to a first lieutenancy and a captaincy, and in his thirty-eighth year he was appointed one of the visitors to West Point, whose duty it was to inspect the Academy and report at stated intervals on its condition. This appointment, insignificant in itself, is notable because it marks the point at which the trails of Grant and Lee first approach each other, for at the time that Captain Lee was serving as an official visitor, Ulysses Grant was attempting to secure an assistant professorship at West Point.

Chapter IV
The Boyhood of Grant

Deerfield, Ohio, was not a place of any importance when Captain Noah Grant of Bunker Hill fame arrived there from the East. Indeed, it was not then much more than a spot on the map and it has ever won any great renown. Yet in this tiny Ohio village there lived at one and the same time Owen Brown, the father of John Brown, who virtually began the Civil War, and Jesse Grant, the father of Ulysses Grant, who practically brought it to a close.

It is certainly strange that these two men should, with all the world to choose from, have chanced upon the same obscure little village, but it is still stranger that one of them should have become the employer of the other and that they should both have lived in the very same house. Such, however, is the fact, for when Jesse Grant first began to earn his living as a tanner, he worked for and boarded with Owen Brown, little dreaming that his son and his employer's son would some day shake the world.

It was not at Deerfield, however, but at Point Pleasant, Ohio, that Jesse Grant's distinguished son was born on April 27, 1822, in a cottage not much larger than the cabin in which Abraham Lincoln first saw the light. Mr. and Mrs. Grant and other members of their family differed among themselves as to what the boy should be called, but they settled the question by each writing his or her favorite name on a slip of paper and then depositing all the slips in a hat, with the understanding that the child should receive the first two names drawn from that receptacle. This resulted in the selection of Hiram and Ulysses, and the boy was accordingly called Hiram Ulysses Grant until the United States government re-christened him in a curious fashion many years later. To his immediate family, however, he was always known as Ulysses, which his playmates soon twisted into the nickname "Useless," more or less good-naturedly applied.

Grant's father moved to Georgetown, Ohio, soon after his son's birth, and there his boyhood days were passed. The place was not at that time much more than a frontier village and its inhabitants were mostly pioneers--not the adventurous, exploring pioneers who discover new countries, but the hardy advance-guard of civilization, who clear the forests and transform the wilderness into farming land. Naturally, there was no culture and very little education among these people. They were a sturdy, self-respecting, hard-working lot, of whom every man was the equal of every other, and to whom riches and poverty were alike unknown. In a community of this sort there was, of course, no pampering of the children, and if there had been, Grant's parents would probably have been the last to indulge in it. His father, Jesse Grant, was a stern and very busy man who had neither the time nor the inclination to coddle the boy, and his mother, absorbed in her household duties and the care of a numerous family, gave him only such attention as was necessary to keep him in good health. Young Ulysses was, therefore, left to his own devices almost as soon as he could toddle, and he quickly became self-reliant to a degree that alarmed the neighbors. Indeed, some of them rushed into the house one morning shouting that the boy was out in the barn swinging himself on the farm horses' tails and in momentary danger of being kicked to pieces; but Mrs. Grant received the announcement with perfect calmness, feeling sure that Ulysses would not amuse himself in that way unless he knew the animals thoroughly understood what he was doing.

Certainly this confidence in the boy's judgment was entirely justified as far as horses were concerned, for they were the joy of his life and he was never so happy as when playing or working in or about the stables. Indeed, he was not nine years old when he began to handle a team in the fields. From that time forward he welcomed every duty that involved riding, driving or caring for horses, and shirked every other sort of work about the farm and tannery. Fortunately, there was plenty of employment for him in the line of carting materials or driving the hay wagons and harrows, and his father, finding that he could be trusted with such duties, allowed him, before he reached his teens, to drive a 'bus or stage between Georgetown and the neighboring villages entirely by himself. In fact, he was given such free use of the horses that when it became necessary for him to help in the tannery, he would take a team and do odd jobs for the neighbors until he earned enough, with the aid of the horses, to hire a boy to take his place in the hated tan-yard.

This and other work was, of course, only done out of school hours, for his parents sent him as early as possible to a local "subscription" school, which he attended regularly for many years. "Spare the rod and spoil the child" was one of the maxims of the school, and the first duty of the boys on assembling each morning was to gather a good-sized bundle of beech-wood switches, of which the schoolmaster made such vigorous use that before the sessions ended the supply was generally exhausted. Grant received his fair share of this discipline, but as he never resented it, he doubtless got no more of it than he deserved and it probably did him good.

Among his schoolmates he had the reputation of talking less than any of the other boys and of knowing more about horses than all of them put together. An opportunity to prove this came when he was about eleven, for a circus appeared in the village with a trick pony, and during the performance the clown offered five dollars to any boy who could ride him. Several of Ulysses' friends immediately volunteered, but he sat quietly watching the fun while one after another of the boys fell victim to the pony's powers. Finally, when the little animal's triumph seemed complete, Grant stepped into the ring and sprang upon his back. A tremendous tussle for the mastery immediately ensued, but though he reared and shied and kicked, the tricky little beast was utterly unable to throw its fearless young rider, and amid the shouts of the audience the clown at last stopped the contest and paid Ulysses the promised reward.

From that time forward his superiority as a horseman was firmly established, and as he grew older and his father allowed him to take longer and longer trips with the teams, he came to be the most widely traveled boy in the village. Indeed, he was only about fifteen when he covered nearly a hundred and fifty miles in the course of one of his journeys, taking as good care of his horses as he did of himself, and transacting the business entrusted to him with entire satisfaction to all concerned. These long, and often lonely, trips increased his independence and so encouraged his habit of silence that many of the village people began to think him a dunce.

His father, however, was unmistakably proud of the quiet boy who did what he was told to do without talking about it, and though he rarely displayed his feelings, the whole village knew that he thought "Useless" was a wonder and smiled at his parental pride. But the smile almost turned to a laugh when it became known that he proposed to send the boy to West Point, for the last cadet appointed from Georgetown had failed in his examinations before he had been a year at the Academy, and few of the neighbors believed that Ulysses would survive as long. Certainly, the boy himself had never aspired to a cadetship, and when his father suddenly remarked to him one morning that he was likely to obtain the appointment, he receive the announcement with uncomprehending surprise.

"What appointment?" he asked

"To West Point," replied his father. "I have applied for it."

"But I won't go!" gasped the astonished youth.

"I think you will," was the quiet but firm response, and Grant, who had been taught obedience almost from his cradle, decided that if his father thought so, he did, too.

But, though the young man yielded to his parent's wishes, he had no desire to become a soldier and entirely agreed with the opinion of the village that he had neither the ability nor the education to acquit himself with credit. In fact, the whole idea of military life was so distasteful to him that he almost hoped he would not fulfill the physical and other requirements for admission. Indeed, the only thought that reconciled him to the attempt was that it necessitated a trip from Ohio to New York, which gratified his longing to see more of the world. This was so consoling that it was almost with a gay heart that he set out of the Hudson in the middle of May, 1839.

For a boy who had lived all his life in an inland village on the outskirts of civilization the journey was absolutely adventurous, for although he was then in his eighteenth year, he had never even as much as seen a railroad and his experiences on the cars, canal boats and steamers were all delightfully surprising. Therefore, long as the journey was, it was far too short for him, and on May 25th he reached his destination. Two lonely and homesick weeks followed, and then, much to his astonishment and somewhat to his regret, he received word that he had passed the examination for admission and was a full-fledged member of the cadet corps of West Point.

Chapter V
Grant at West Point

Grant's father had obtained his son's appointment to the Academy through the intervention of a member of Congress, who, remembering that the boy was known as Ulysses and that his mother's name before her marriage was Simpson, had written to the Secretary of War at Washington, requesting a cadetship for U. S. Grant. This mistake in his initials was not discovered until the young man presented himself at West Point, but when he explained that his name was Hiram Ulysses Grant and not U. S. Grant, the officials would not correct the error. The Secretary of War had appointed U. S. Grant to the Academy and U. S. Grant was the only person they would officially recognize without further orders. They, therefore, intimated that he could either enroll himself as U. S. Grant or stay out of the Academy, making it quite plain that they cared very little which course he adopted. Confronted with this situation, he signed the enlistment paper as U. S. Grant and the document, bearing his name, which thus became his, can be seen to-day among the records at West Point. This re-christening, of course, supplied his comrades with endless suggestions for nicknames and they immediately interpreted his new initials to suit themselves. "United States," "Under Sized" and "Uncle Sam" all seemed to be appropriate, but the last was the favorite until the day arrived when a more significant meaning was found in "Unconditional Surrender" Grant.

The restrictions and discipline of West Point bore much more harshly on country-bred boys in those years than they do to-day when so many schools prepare students for military duties. But to a green lad like Grant, who had been exceptionally independent all his life, the preliminary training was positive torture. It was then that his habitual silence stood him in good stead, for a talkative, argumentative boy could never have survived the breaking-in process which eventually transformed him from a slouchy bumpkin into a smart, soldier-like young fellow who made the most of his not excessive inches. Still, he hated almost every moment of his first year and ardently hoped that the bill for abolishing the Academy, which was under discussion in Congress, would become a law and enable him to return home without disgrace. But no such law was passed and more experience convinced him that West Point was a very valuable institution which should be strengthened rather than abolished. He had not reached this conclusion, however, at the time of his first furlough, and when he returned to his more and found that his father had procured a fine horse for his exclusive use during his holiday, it was hard to tear himself away and resume his duties. Nevertheless, he did so; and, considering the fact that he was not fond of studying, he made fair progress, especially in mathematics, never reaching the head of his class, but never quite sinking to the bottom. Indeed, if he had not been careless in the matter of incurring demerits from small infractions of the rules, he might have attained respectable, if not high rank in the corps, for he was a clean living, clean spoken boy, without a vicious trait of any kind. Even as it was, he became a sergeant, but inattention to details of discipline finally cost him his promotion and reduced him again to the ranks. At no time, however, did he acquire any real love for the military profession. His sole ambition was to pass the examinations and retire from the service as soon as he could obtain a professorship at some good school or college. At this, he might easily have succeeded with his unmistakable talent for mathematics, and it is even conceivable that he might have qualified as a drawing master or an architect, if not as an artist, for he was fond of sketching and some of his works in this line which have been preserved shows a surprisingly artistic touch.

Graduation day at the Academy brought no distinguished honors to Grant, where he stood twenty-first in a class of thirty-nine, but it did win him one small triumph. As almost everyone knows, the West Point cadets are trained for all arms of the service, sometimes doing duty as infantry, sometimes as artillery and at other times acting as engineers or cavalry; and during the closing week of the year, they give public exhibitions of their proficiency before the official visitors. On this particular occasion the cavalry drill was held in the great riding hall, and after the whole corps had completed their evolutions and were formed in line ready to be dismissed, the commanding officer ordered an extraordinarily high hurdle to be placed in position, and while the great throng of spectators were wondering what this meant they heard the sharp command, "Cadet Grant."

A young man of slight stature, not weighing more than a hundred and twenty pounds, and mounted on a powerful chestnut horse, sprang from the ranks with a quick salute, dashed to the further end of the hall and, swinging his mount about, faced the hurdle. There was a moment's pause and then the rider, putting spurs to his steed, rushed him straight at the obstruction and, lifting him in masterly fashion, cleared the bar as though he and the animal were one. A thunder of applause followed as the horseman quietly resumed his place in the ranks, and after the corps had been dismissed Grant was sought out and congratulated on his remarkable feat. But his response was characteristic of the boy that was, and the man that was to be. "Yes, 'York' is a wonderfully good horse," was all he said.

A lieutenancy in the engineers or cavalry was more than a man of low standing in the Academy could expect, and Grant was assigned to the Fourth Infantry, with orders to report for duty at Jefferson Barracks, St. Louis, Missouri, at the end of a short leave of absence. The prospect of active service, far from his native state, was anything but pleasing to the new officer; but he had come home with a bad cough, and had he not been ordered to the South, it is highly probable that he would have fallen a victim to consumption, of which two of his uncles had already died. The air of Camp Salubrity, Louisiana, where his regiment was quartered, and the healthy, outdoor life, however, quickly checked the disease, and at the end of two years he had acquired a constitution of iron.

Meanwhile, he had met Miss Julia Dent, the sister of one of his classmates whose home was near St. Louis, and had written to the Professor of Mathematics at West Point, requesting his aid in securing an appointment there as his assistant, to which application he received a most encouraging reply. Doubtless, his courtship of Miss Dent made him doubly anxious to realize his long-cherished plan of settling down to the quiet life of a professor. But all hope of this was completely shattered by the orders of the Fourth Infantry which directed it to proceed at once to Texas. Long before the regiment marched, however, he was engaged to "the girl he left behind him" and, although his dream of an instructorship at West Point had vanished, he probably did not altogether abandon his ambition for a career at teaching. But

Fate had other plans for him as he journeyed toward Mexico, where the war clouds were gathering. Lee was moving in the same direction and their trails were soon to merge at the siege of Vera Cruz.

Chapter VI
Lieutenant Grant Under Fire

The movement of the United States troops towards Mexico did not take the country by surprise. It was the direct result of the action of Congress admitting Texas to the Union. Ever since it had won its independence from Mexico, Texas had been seeking to become part of the United States; but there had been violent objection in the North to the admission of any new slave state, and this opposition had effectually prevented its annexation. At the last election (1844), however, a majority of the voters apparently favored the admission of Texas, which was accordingly received into the Union, and the long-standing dispute which it had waged with Mexico as to its proper boundaries was assumed by the United States.

Texas claimed to own far more territory than Mexico was willing to concede, but the facts might easily have been ascertained had the United States government desired to avoid a war. Unfortunately, it had no such desire, and General Zachary Taylor was soon ordered to occupy the disputed territory with about 3,000 men. This force, of which Grant's regiment formed a part, was called the Army of Observation, but it might better have been called the Army of Provocation, for it was obviously intended to provoke an attack on the part of Mexico and to give the United States an excuse for declaring war and settling the boundary question to suit itself.

Probably, there were not many in the army who thought much about the rights or the wrongs of the impending war. There had been no fighting in the United States for more than thirty years, and most of the officers were more interested in seeing real service in the field than they were in discussing the justice or injustice of the cause. Grant was as anxious for glory as any of his comrades, but he cherished no illusions as to the merits of the dispute in which his country was involved. With the clear vision of the silent man who reads and thinks for himself, he saw through the thinly disguised pretenses of the politicians and, recognizing that force was being used against a weaker nation in order to add more slave states to the Union, he formed a very positive opinion that the war was unjustifiable. But though he was forced to this disagreeable conclusion, the young Lieutenant was not the sort of man to criticize his country once she was attacked, or to shirk his duty as a soldier because he did not agree with his superiors on questions of national policy. He thought and said what he liked in private, but he kept his mouth closed in public, feeling that his duties as an officer were quite sufficient without assuming responsibilities which belonged to the authorities in Washington.

War was inevitable almost from the moment that Texas was annexed, but with full knowledge of this fact neither the President nor Congress made any effective preparations for meeting the impending crisis, and when hostilities actually began, General Taylor was directed to advance under conditions which virtually required him to fight his way to safety. Indeed, he was practically cut off from all hope of reenforcement as soon as the first shot was fired, for his orders obliged him to move into the interior of the country, and had his opponents been properly commanded, they could have overwhelmed him and annihilated his whole force. The very audacity of the little American army, however, seemed to paralyze the Mexicans who practically made no resistance until Taylor reached a place called Palo Alto, which in Spanish means "Tall Trees."

Meanwhile Grant had been made regimental quartermaster, charged with the duty of seeing that the troops were furnished with proper food and caring for all property and supplies. Heartily as he disliked this task, which was not only dull and difficult, but also bade fair to prevent him from taking active part in the prospective battles, he set to work with the utmost energy. By the time the enemy began to dispute the road, he had overcome the immense difficulty of supplying troops on a march through a tropical country and was prepared to take part in any fighting that occurred. But the Mexicans gathered at TALL TREES on May 8, 1846, were not prepared for a serious encounter. They fired at the invaders, but their short-range cannon loaded with solid shot rarely reached the Americans, and when a ball did come rolling towards them on the ground, the troops merely stepped to one side and allowed the missile to pass harmlessly through their opened ranks. After the American artillery reached the field, however, the enemy was driven from its position and the next day the advance was resumed to Resaca de la Palma, where stronger opposition was encountered.

Grant was on the right wing of the army as it pressed forward through dense undergrowth to drive the Mexicans from the coverts in which they had taken shelter. It was impossible to give any exact orders in advancing through this jungle, and the men under Grant's command struggled forward until they reached a clearing where they caught sight of a small body of Mexicans. The young Lieutenant instantly ordered a charge and, dashing across the open ground, captured the party only to discover that they were merely stragglers left behind by other American troops who had already charged over the same ground. No one appreciated the humor of this exploit more than Grant. It reminded him, he said, of the soldier who boasted that he had been in a charge and had cut off the leg of one of the enemy's officers. "Why didn't you cut off his head?" inquired his commander. "Oh, somebody had done that already," replied the valiant hero.

Slight as the fighting was at Resaca, it completely satisfied the Mexicans, and for over three months they left the Americans severely alone. Meanwhile, General Taylor received reenforcements and in August, 1846, he proceeded against the town of Monterey, which the enemy had fortified with considerable skill and where they were evidently prepared to make a desperate resistance. Grant was again quartermaster, and the terrific heat which forced the army to do its marching at night or during the early hours of the morning, greatly increased his labors and severely tested his patience. Almost all the transportation animals were mules, and as very few of them were trained for the work, they were hard to load and even harder to handle after their burdens were adjusted. One refractory animal would often stampede all the rest, scattering provisions and ammunition in their tracks, driving the teamsters to the point of frenzy and generally hurling confusion through the camp. Even Grant, who never uttered an oath in his life, was often sorely tried by these exasperating experiences, but he kept command of his temper and by his quiet persistence brought order out of chaos in spite of beasts and men.

His disappointment was bitter, however, when the attack on Monterey began and he found himself left without any assignment in the field. Lieutenant Meade, destined at a later date to command the Union forces at Gettysburg, was one of the officers entrusted with the preliminary reconnoissance against the city, and when the fighting actually commenced on September 21st, 1846, the deserted Quartermaster mounted his horse and rode to the scene of the action, determined to see something of the battle even if he could not take part in it. He arrived at the moment when his regiment was ordered to charge against what was known as the Black Fort, and dashed forward with his men into the very jaws of death. Certainly "someone had blundered," for the charge which had been intended merely as a feint was carried too far and scores of men were mowed down under the terrible fire of the enemy's guns. Temporary shelter was at last reached, however, and under cover of it the Adjutant borrowed Grant's horse; but he fell soon after the charge was renewed and the Colonel, noticing the impetuous Quartermaster, promptly appointed him to take the fallen officer's place. By this time the troops had fought their way into the town and the enemy, posted in the Plaza or Principal Square, commanded every approach to it. As long as the Americans kept in the side streets they were comparatively safe, but the moment they showed themselves in any of the avenues leading to the Plaza, they encountered a hail of bullets. This was serious enough; but at the end of two days the situation became critical, for the ammunition began to run low, and it was realized that, if the Mexicans discovered this, they would sweep down and cut their defenseless opponents to pieces. Face to face with this predicament, the Colonel on September 23rd, called for a volunteer to carry a dispatch to Headquarters, and Grant instantly responded.

To reach his destination it was necessary to run the gantlet of the enemy, for every opening from the Plaza was completely exposed to their fire. But trusting in the fleetness of his horse, the young lieutenant leaped into the saddle and, swinging himself down, Indian fashion, on one side of his steed so as to shield himself behind its body, he dashed away on his perilous mission. A roar of muskets greeted him at every corner, but he flashed safely by, leaping a high wall which lay across his path and then, speeding straight for the east end of the town, reached the commanding General and reported the peril of his friends.

Meanwhile the Americans began one of the most curious advances ever made by an army, for General Worth, finding that he could not force his troops through the streets leading to the Plaza without great loss of life, ordered them to enter the houses and break down the intervening walls, so that they could pass from one adjoining house to another under cover, directly to the heart of the city. This tunneling maneuver was executed with great skill, and when the walls of the houses nearest the Plaza were reached and masses of men stood ready to pour through the openings into the Square, its astonished defenders gave up the fight and promptly surrendered the city.

Chapter VII
Captain Lee at the Front

Astonishing as General Taylor's success had been, the authorities at Washington decided, largely for political reasons, to appoint a new commander, and three months after the battle of Monterey, General Winfield Scott, the Commander-in-Chief of the United States army, was ordered to the seat of the war.

It would be impossible to imagine two officers more utterly different than Taylor and Scott, but each in his own way exerted a profound influence upon the careers of Grant and Lee. Taylor was a rough, uncultivated man, fearless, shrewd and entirely capable, but with nothing to suggest the soldier in his appearance, dress or dignity. On the contrary, he usually appeared sitting slouchily on some woe-begone old animal, his long legs dangling on one side of the saddle, the bridle rein looped over his arm and a straw hat on his head, more like a ploughman than an officer of high rank. Indeed, he seldom donned a uniform of any description, and his only known appearance in full dress occurred during an official meeting with an admiral, when, out of regard for naval etiquette, he attired himself in his finest array. But this effort at politeness was not calculated to encourage him, for the admiral, knowing his host's objection to uniforms, had been careful to leave his on his ship and appeared in civilian attire.

Scott, on the other hand, was a fussy and rather pompous individual, who delighted in brass buttons and gold lace and invariably presented a magnificent appearance. But, like Taylor, he was an excellent officer and thoroughly competent to handle an army in the field. He was, moreover, entirely familiar with the material of which the American army was composed, and his first move on assuming command was to order practically all the regular United States troops and their officers to join him near Vera Cruz, leaving Taylor virtually nothing but volunteer regiments. The Fourth Infantry accordingly parted with its old commander and reported to Scott, where it was assigned to the division of General Worth, and for the first time Grant met many of the men with and against whom he was to be thrown during the Civil War.

It was certainly a remarkable body of officers that Scott gathered about him at the outset of his campaign, for it included such men as Stonewall Jackson, Jefferson Davis, McClellan, Joseph Johnson, Jubal Early, A. P. Hill, Meade, Beauregard, Hooker, Longstreet, Hancock, Thomas and, last but not least, Ulysses Grant and Robert Lee. Lee had arrived in Mexico soon after the battle of Monterey, but he had no opportunity for distinction until the spring of 1847, when preparations were begun for the siege of Vera Cruz. He had, however, already demonstrated his ability as an engineer, and with Lieutenant Beauregard who, fourteen years later, commanded the attack on Fort Sumter, he was entrusted with posting the American batteries at Vera Cruz. This he did to such advantage that they made short work of the city which fell into the invaders' hands, March 29, 1847, after a week's siege. Scott was quick to recognize the merit of officers, and Lee was straightway attached to his personal staff, with the result that when the army began its forward movement most of the difficult and delicate work was confided to his care.

Scott's object was the capture of the City of Mexico, the capital of the Republic, and against this stronghold he moved with energy and skill. At Cerro Gordo the Mexicans opposed him with considerable force, but maneuvers, suggested by Lee, enabled him to outflank the enemy and drive them, without much trouble, from his path. Again at Contreras a check occurred, part of the army having advanced over a well-nigh impassable country and lost touch with the Commander-in-Chief. One after another seven officers were dispatched to carry the necessary orders, but all returned without effecting their purpose. But at midnight, in the midst of a torrential storm Lee arrived from the front, having overcome all difficulties--an achievement which Scott subsequently described as "the greatest feat of physical and moral courage performed by any individual in my knowledge, pending the campaign."

But Lee was more than merely brave and daring. He was thorough. When work was entrusted to his care he performed it personally, never relying on others further than was absolutely necessary, and never resting satisfied until he was certain that he had accomplished his task. On one of his most important reconnoissances he rode into the interior of the country at night to locate the position of the enemy, and after he had proceeded a considerable distance his guide informed him that if he went any further he would be a prisoner, for the whole Mexican army lay directly in his path. He, accordingly, advanced more cautiously, but the guide again begged him to halt, declaring that he could already see the enemies' tents lying on the hillside below. Peering through the darkness in the direction indicated, Lee discovered what appeared to be an encampment of many thousand men, and for the moment he was tempted to accept his companion's conclusion that this was the main force of the Mexicans. Second thoughts, however, convinced him that he ought not to make a report based upon the eyes of the guide, and, despite the man's frightened protests, he decided to stay where he was and see the situation for himself by daylight. But, before the morning fairly dawned, it was apparent that the supposed army of Mexicans was nothing but a huge flock of sheep and, galloping back with the news that the road was clear, he led a troop of cavalry forward and located the enemy posted many miles away in an entirely different position.

The Mexicans stubbornly, though unsuccessfully, resisted the American army as it pushed toward their capital, and in the battles which ensued Lee was so active that his gallant conduct was praised in almost every dispatch of his Chief, who subsequently attributed much of his success "to the skill and valor of Robert E. Lee," whom he did not hesitate to describe as "the greatest military genius in America." Continuous praise from such a source would have been more than sufficient to turn the average officer's head, but Lee continued to perform his duties without showing the least sign of vanity or conceit. Quiet, thoughtful, quick to take advantage of any opportunity, but greedy of neither honors nor personal distinction of any kind, he won the admiration of his comrades as well as the confidence of his superiors, and his promotion, first to the rank of major and then to that of lieutenant-colonel, was universally approved.

Meanwhile, Grant had been acquitting himself with high credit in all the work which fell to his share. He was in no position to render service of anything like the importance of Lee's, but he did what he was ordered to do and did it well, being brevetted a first lieutenant for conspicuous gallantry at the battle of Molino del Rey, September 8, 1847. Again, on September 13, in the fighting around Chapultepec, where Lee, though wounded, remained in the saddle until he fell fainting from his horse, Grant gained considerable distinction by his quick action in relieving a dangerous pressure on part of the American lines by posting a small gun in the belfry of a church and galling the enemy with his deadly accurate fire. It was characteristic of the man that when complimented upon this achievement and told that a second gun would be sent to him, Grant merely saluted. He might, with truth, have informed his commanding officer that the belfry could not accommodate another gun, but it was not his habit to talk when there was no need of it, or to question the wisdom of his superior officer. He, therefore, quietly accepted the praise and the superfluous gun and, returning to his post, resumed his excellent service. This and other similar conduct won him further promotion, and on September 14, 1847, when the Americans marched triumphantly into the Mexican capital, he was brevetted a captain.

The war practically ended with this event and within a year Grant was married to Miss Julia Dent and stationed at Sackett's Harbor, New York, while Lee was assigned to the defenses of Baltimore, not far from his old home.

Chapter VIII
Colonel Lee After the Mexican War

It is probable that Lee would have been well content to remain indefinitely at Baltimore, for his duties there enabled him to be more with his family than had been possible for some years. To his boys and girls he was both a companion and a friend and in their company he took the keenest delight. In fact, he and his wife made their home the center of attraction for all the young people of the neighborhood, and no happier household existed within the confines of their beloved Virginia.

It was not to be expected, however, that an officer of Lee's reputation would be allowed to remain long in obscurity, and in 1852, he was appointed Superintendent at West Point. A wiser selection for this important post could scarcely have been made, for Colonel Lee, then in his forty-sixth year, possessed rare qualifications for the duties entrusted to his charge. He was not only a man whose splendid presence, magnificent physique and distinguished record were certain to win the admiration and respect of young men, but he combined in his character and temperament all the qualities of a tactful teacher and an inspiring leader. Quiet and dignified, but extremely sympathetic, he governed the cadets without seeming to command them and, as at his own home, he exerted a peculiarly happy influence upon all with whom he came into personal contact. Among the cadets during his service at West Point were J. E. B. Stuart, who was to prove himself one of the greatest cavalry leaders that this country has ever produced, and his elder son, Custis Lee, who, improving on his father's almost perfect record, graduated first in his class.

About this time certain important changes were effected in the organization of the regular army, and the popular Superintendent of West Point was immediately appointed Lieutenant-Colonel of the newly formed Second Cavalry, with orders to proceed to Texas and protect the settlers against the attacks of hostile Indians. It was with keen regret that Lee received this assignment, for, though intended as a promotion, it removed him from the corps of engineers to which he had always been attached and obliged him to break all his home ties for what was practically police duty in the wilderness. Nevertheless, no thought of resigning from the army apparently crossed his mind. He soon joined his regiment in Texas, where, for almost three years, he patrolled the country, ruling the Indians by diplomacy or force, as occasion required, practically living in the saddle and experiencing all the discomforts and privations of garrison life at an outpost of civilization.

Almost his only relaxation during this lonely and exhausting service was his correspondence with his wife and children, and his letters to them, written in rough camps and on the march, show that his thoughts were constantly with his home and loved ones. "It has been said that our letters are good representations of our minds," he wrote his youngest daughter from Texas in 1857; and certainly Lee's correspondence, exhibiting as it does, consideration for others, modesty, conscientiousness, affection and a spirit of fun, affords an admirable reflection of the writer.

"Did I tell you that 'Jim Nooks,' Mrs. Waite's cat, was dead?" he wrote one of his girls. "He died of apoplexy. I foretold his end. Coffee and cream for breakfast, pound cake for lunch, turtle and oysters for dinner, buttered toast for tea and Mexican rats, taken raw, for supper! He grew enormously and ended in a spasm. His beauty could not save him.... But I saw 'cats as is cats' at Sarassa.... The entrance of Madame [his hostess] was foreshadowed by the coming in of her stately cats with visages grim and tails erect, who preceded, surrounded and followed her. They are of French breed and education, and when the claret and water were poured out for my refreshment they jumped on the table for a sit-to.... I had to leave the wild-cat on the Rio Grande; he was too savage and had grown as large as a small sized dog. He would pounce on a kid as Tom Tita [his daughter's cat] would on a mouse and would whistle like a tiger when you approached him."

But it was not always in this chatty fashion that he wrote, for in 1856, when the question of slavery was being fiercely discussed throughout the country, he expressed his views on the subject with a moderation and broadmindedness exceedingly rare in those excited times.

"In this enlightened age," he wrote his wife, "there are few, I believe, but will acknowledge that slavery as an institution is a moral and political evil in any country. I think it, however, a greater evil to the white than to the black race; and while my feelings are strongly interested in behalf of the latter, my sympathies are stronger for the former. The blacks are immeasurably better off here than in Africa--morally, socially and physically. The painful discipline they are undergoing is necessary for their instruction as a race and I hope it will prepare and lead them to better things. How long this subjection may be necessary is known and ordered by a wise and merciful Providence. Their emancipation will sooner result from a mild and melting influence than from the storms and contests of fiery controversy. This influence though slow is sure."

Such were the views of Robert Lee on this great question of the day, and even as he wrote the country was beginning to notice a country lawyer named Abraham Lincoln, who was expressing almost identically the same opinions in no uncertain terms.

But the calm advice of Lincoln and Lee did not appeal to the hot-heads who were for abolishing slavery instantly at any and every cost. In October, 1859, when Lee was on a short visit to Arlington, John Brown, whose father had once lived with Grant's father, attempted to take the whole matter into his already blood-stained hands. It is a strange coincidence that Lee should have chanced to be in Virginia just at this particular crisis, and still stranger that the errand which had called him home should have related to the emancipation of slaves. But the facts were that Mr. Custis, his father-in-law, had died a few weeks previously, leaving him as the executor of his will, which provided, among other things, for the gradual emancipation of all his slaves. Lee had accordingly obtained leave of absence to make a flying trip to Virginia for the purpose of undertaking this duty, and he was actually making arrangements to carry out Mr. Custis's wishes in respect to his slaves when the news of John Brown's raid on Harper's Ferry reached Arlington. Word of this reckless attempt to free the slaves by force reached him in the form of a dispatch from the Secretary of War, ordering him to take immediate charge of the United States marines who were being hurried to the scene of action. He instantly obeyed and, with Lieutenant J. E. B. Stuart as his second in command, hastened to Harper's Ferry and, directing his troops to storm the engine-house where Brown and his followers had taken refuge, effected their capture almost without striking a blow. Then, after delivering his prisoners to the proper authorities, he completed his work at Arlington and returned to Texas and the rough life of guarding the frontier line.

From this duty he was recalled to Washington in March, 1861, when the Southern States were rapidly forming the Confederacy, the whole country was in wild confusion and the nation was facing the prospect of a terrific civil war.

Chapter IX
Captain Grant in a Hard Fight

Meanwhile, what had become of Grant? The War Department did not know and apparently did not care. Jefferson Davis, the Secretary of War, responded to his father's anxious inquiry that Captain U. S. Grant had resigned from the army in July, 1854, but that he had no official knowledge as to why he had taken this action. Mr. Grant, however, soon learned the facts from other sources, and in his bitter disappointment was heard to exclaim that "West Point had ruined one of his boys for him."

It was natural enough that the stern and proud old gentleman should have blamed West Point for the heart-breaking failure of his favorite son, but, as a matter of fact, West Point was in no way responsible for what had occurred. Neither during his cadetship at the Academy nor for some years after his graduation from that institution had Ulysses Grant touched wine or stimulants in any form. He had, indeed, tried to learn to smoke during his West Point days but had merely succeeded in making himself ill. During his hard campaigning in Mexico, however, he had learned not only to smoke, but to drink, though it was not until some years after the war closed that he began to indulge to excess. As a matter of fact, he ought never to have touched a drop of any intoxicant, for a very little was always too much for him, and the result was that he soon came to be known in the army as a drinking man. Had he been at home, surrounded by his wife and children and busily engaged, perhaps he might not have yielded to his weakness. But his orders carried him to lonely posts on the Pacific, many hundreds of miles away from his family, with no duties worthy of the name, and the habit grew on him until the exasperated Colonel of his regiment at last gave him the choice of resigning or being court-martialed for conduct unbecoming an officer and a gentleman. Face to face with this ugly alternative, he chose resignation, and the army, officially, knew him no more.

It was not only social and professional disgrace, but financial ruin which confronted the broken officer as he bade good-bye to his regiment at its desolate quarters in California, after fifteen years of service to the army. He was absolutely without money and, at the age of thirty-two, it was by no means easy for him to begin life all over again and earn his own living at a new calling. His fellow officers provided him with enough cash for his immediate wants, and with their help he managed to find his way back to Sackett's Harbor, New York, where there was a little money owing him. But he failed to collect this and remained hopelessly stranded until another officer came to his rescue and provided him with sufficient funds to take him to his home. This friend in time of need was Simon B. Buckner, whom he was to meet again under strange and dramatic circumstances.

It was hardly to be expected, under such conditions, that stern old Jesse Grant would welcome the home-coming of his eldest son. Nevertheless, he helped him on his way to his wife and children, and, sick at heart and broken in health, the young man joined his family and began a desperate struggle to earn his own living. Mrs. Grant's father was a slave owner and a sympathizer with the South in the growing trouble between that section of the country and the North. But the quarrel had not yet reached the breaking point, and although he did not approve of his son-in-law's northern views and heartily disapproved of his conduct, he gave him a start as a farmer and then left him to work out his own salvation.

Farming was the only occupation at which Grant could hope to make a living, but he soon found that he did not know enough about this to make a success of it, and gradually fell back on his youthful experience as a teamster, hauling wood to the city where he sold it to the railroad or to anyone that would buy. At this he was fairly successful and, encouraged by his wife who stood bravely by him, he built a house with his own hands, which, although it was not much more than a log cabin, was sufficiently large to shelter his small family. All this time he was making a hard fight to conquer his drinking habits, but the vice had taken a terrible hold on him and he could not easily shake it off. It was only a matter of time, therefore, before his experiment at farming failed and with the aid of his father-in-law he entered business as a real estate broker in St. Louis. But for this calling he had no qualification whatsoever, and after a disheartening experience in attempting to secure the post of county engineer, he accepted his father's suggestion that he join his brothers in the leather business in Galena, Illinois, and retired there with his family in the spring of 1860.

The position which his father had made for him was not much more than a clerkship and the work was dull for a man who had been accustomed to active, outdoor life; but he was received with tact and kindness, no reference was made to his past record of failure and all this helped him to continue the successful struggle which he was making to regain control of himself and his habits.

Indeed, from the time he began his residence in Galena he already had the battle well in hand and he fought it out with such grim resolution that before a year had passed his victory was complete. Scarcely anyone in the little town knew of this silent struggle for self-mastery. Indeed, very few people knew anything at all about the newcomer, save that he was a quiet, hard-working man who occasionally appeared on the streets wearing a blue army overcoat which had seen rough service. This weather-stained garment, however, forced Grant to break his habitual silence, for he fully shared General Taylor's prejudice against a uniform and felt obliged to apologize for wearing even part of one. So one day he explained to a neighbor that he wore the coat because it was made of good material and he thought he ought to use it as long as it lasted. That was all the citizens of Galena then learned of the record of the man who had served with high honor in well-nigh every battle of the Mexican War. Had it depended upon him, their information would probably have begun and ended there.

During all this time the feeling between the North and the South was growing more and more bitter, but Galena was a town divided against itself on the slavery question. Grant himself was a Democrat. If he was not in favor of slavery, he certainly was not opposed to it, for he favored Douglas and not Lincoln in the contest for the Presidency, and Douglas was strongly against any interference with slavery. Indeed, it is a curious coincidence that at or about the time when Lee's family was ceasing to own slaves, Grant's family acquired some. Such, however, is the fact, for on the death of her father, Mrs. Grant inherited several Negroes and there is some evidence that Grant himself sold or attempted to sell them.

But, though he was at that time no champion of the black race, Grant was always a strong Union man, opposed heart and soul to secession. Indeed, when news of the attack upon Fort Sumter arrived in Galena, he arrayed himself with the defenders of the flag gathered at a mass meeting held in the town to form a company in response to the President's call for 75,000 volunteers. Moreover, this meeting had no sooner been called to order than someone proposed him as chairman, and to his utter astonishment, he found himself pushed from the rear of the room to the front and from the front to the platform. Probably few in the audience knew who or what he was, and his embarrassment was such that for a few minutes no words came to his lips. Finally, however, he managed to announce the object of the meeting, warning those who intended to enlist that they would be engaged in serious business involving hard work and privation, expressing his willingness to aid in forming the Galena Company and ending with a simple statement of his own intention to reenter the army.

There was nothing eloquent about his short speech but it had the tone of a man who knew what he was talking about, and the audience, availing itself of his military experience, immediately voted to entrust the organization and drilling of the volunteers to his care, and from that moment he never again entered his father's place of business.

Chapter X
Grant's Difficulties in Securing a Command

The command of the local company was, of course, offered to Grant as soon as it was formed, but he declined, believing himself qualified for somewhat higher rank than a captaincy of volunteers. Nevertheless, he did all he could to prepare the recruits for active service in the field and when they were ordered to Springfield, the capital of Illinois, he journeyed there to see them properly mustered into the service of the state.

Springfield was a hubbub of noise and a rallying point for well-meaning incompetence when he arrived upon the scene. New officers in new uniforms swaggered in every public meeting place, bands of music played martial airs at every street corner and volunteers sky-larked and paraded in all sorts of impossible uniforms and with every form of theatric display. But system and order were absolutely lacking, and the adjutant-general's office, littered with blanks and well-nigh knee deep with papers, was the most helpless spot in the welter of confusion. All the material for a respectable army was at hand, but how to form it into an effective force was more than anyone seemed to know. The mass of military forms and blanks intended for that purpose was mere waste paper in the hands of the amiable but ignorant insurance agent who bore the title of adjutant-general, and no one of the patriotic mob had sufficient knowledge to instruct him in his duties. In the midst of all this hopeless confusion, however, someone suggested that a man by the name of Grant, who had come down with the Galena Company, had been in the army and ought to know about such things. The Governor accordingly sought out "the man from Galena" just as he was starting for his home, with the result that he was soon at a desk in the adjutant's office, filling out the necessary papers at three dollars a day, while the brand new captains, colonels and generals posed in the foreground to the tune of popular applause.

From this time forward order gradually took the place of chaos and the political generals and comic-opera soldiers were slowly shifted from the scene. But scarcely anyone noticed the silent man, hard at work in his shirt sleeves in a corner of the adjutant's room, and such inquiries as were made concerning him elicited the information that he was a cast-off of the regular army, with a dubious reputation for sobriety, who had been hired as a clerk. But the Governor of Illinois was an intelligent man, and he was well aware of the service which the ex-Captain of regulars was performing for the State, and on the completion of his work in the adjutant's office Grant was given a nominal title and assigned to visit the various regiments at their encampments to see that they were properly mustered in. He, accordingly, straightway set to work at this task, and his brisk, business-like manner of handling it made an impression upon those with whom he came in contact, for one of the temporary camps became known as Camp Grant.

Meanwhile, seeing his duties coming to an end without much hope of further employment, he wrote the following letter to the Adjutant-General of the United States Army at Washington:

"Sir:

"Having served for fifteen years in the regular army, including four years at West Point, and feeling it the duty of every one who has been educated at the Government expense to offer their services for the support of that Government, I have the honor, very respectfully, to tender my services until the close of the war in such capacity as may be offered. I would say in view of my present age and length of service, I feel myself competent to command a regiment, if the President, in his judgment, should see fit to entrust one to me. Since the first call of the President I have been serving on the staff of the Governor of this State, rendering such aid as I could in the organization of our State militia, and am still engaged in that capacity. A letter addressed to me at Springfield, Ill., will reach me."

But the authorities at Washington took no notice whatsoever of this modest letter, which was evidently tossed aside and completely forgotten. Indeed, it was so completely buried in the files of the War Department that it disappeared for years and, when it was at last discovered, the war was a thing of the past.

This silent rebuff was enough to discourage any sensitive man and Grant felt it keenly, but he did not entirely despair of accomplishing his end. He tried to gain an interview with General Fremont who was stationed in a neighboring state and, failing in this, sought out McClellan, his comrade in the Mexican War, who had been made a major-general and was then in the vicinity of Covington, Kentucky, where Grant had gone to visit his parents. But McClellan either would not or could not see him. Indeed, he had about reached the conclusion that his quest was hopeless, when he happened to meet a friend who offered to tell the Governor of Ohio that he wished to reenter the army, with the result that before long he was tendered the colonelcy of an Ohio regiment. In the meantime, however, he had unexpectedly received a telegram from the Governor of Illinois, appointing him to the command of the 21st Illinois regiment, and this he had instantly accepted. Had he known the exact circumstances under which this post was offered him, perhaps he might not have acted so promptly, but he knew enough to make him aware that the appointment was not altogether complimentary and it is quite likely that he would have accepted it in any event.

The facts were, however, that the Colonel of the 21st Regiment had proved to be an ignorant and bombastic adventurer, who had appeared before his troops clothed in a ridiculous costume and armed like a pirate king, and there was such dissatisfaction among both the officers and men that a new commander was urgently demanded. Of this Grant already knew something, but he was not advised that the regiment had become so utterly demoralized by its incompetent leader that it was nothing less than a dangerous and unruly mob, of which the Governor could not induce any self-respecting officer to take charge. He had, indeed, offered the command to at least half a dozen other men before he tendered it to Grant, and he must have been intensely relieved to receive his prompt acceptance.

The new Colonel did not wait to procure a new uniform before reporting for duty, but, hastening to the Fair Grounds close to Springfield where his troops were stationed, ordered them to assemble for inspection. But incompetent leadership had played havoc with the discipline of the regiment, and the men shambled from their tents without any attempt at military formation, more from curiosity than in obedience to orders.

The new Colonel stepped to the front, wearing a rusty suit of civilian's clothes, his trousers tucked into his dusty boots, a battered hat on his head, a bandanna handkerchief tied around his waist in place of a sash and carrying a stick in place of a sword. Altogether he presented a most unimpressive figure and it would not have been surprising if a wild guffaw of laughter had greeted him, but the troops, studying his strong, calm face, contented themselves with calling for a speech. Then they waited in silence for his response and they did not have to wait long.

"Men!" he commanded sharply. "Go to your quarters!"

The regiment fairly gasped its astonishment. It had never heard a speech like that before and, taken completely by surprise, it moved quietly from the field.

Sentries were instantly posted, camp limits established and preparations made for enforcing strict discipline. It was not to be supposed that such prompt reforms would pass unchallenged, but arrests followed the first signs of disobedience and punishment swiftly followed the arrests.

"For every minute I'm kept here I'll have an ounce of your blood!" threatened a dangerous offender whom the Colonel had ordered to be tied up.

"Gag that man!" was the quiet response. "And when his time is up I'll cut him loose myself."

Before night, all was quiet in the camp of the 21st Regiment of Illinois Volunteers.

Grant was in command.

Chapter XI
Lee at the Parting of the Ways

While Grant was thus striving to reenter the army, Lee was having a struggle of a very different sort. Summoned from his distant post in Texas, where only an occasional rumble of the coming tempest reached his ears, he suddenly found himself in the center of the storm which threatened to wreck the Republic. In the far South seven states had already seceded; in Washington, Congressmen, Senators, and members of the Cabinet were abandoning their posts; in the army and navy his friends were daily tendering their resignations; and his own state, divided between love for the Union and sympathy with its neighbors, was hovering on the brink of secession.

The issue in Lee's mind was not the existence of slavery. He had long been in favor of emancipation, and Virginia had more than once come so close to abolishing slavery by law that its disappearance from her borders was practically assured within a very short period. All his own slaves he had long since freed and he was gradually emancipating his father-in-law's, according to the directions of Mr. Custis's will. But the right of each state to govern itself without interference from the Federal Government seemed to Lee essential to the freedom of the people. He recognized, however, that secession was revolution and, calmly and conscientiously examining the question, he concluded that, if force were used to compel any state to remain in the Union, resistance would be justifiable. Most Virginians reached this decision impulsively, light-heartedly, defiantly or vindictively, and more or less angrily, according to their temperaments and the spirit of the times, but not so Lee. He unaffectedly prayed God for guidance in the struggle between his patriotism and his devotion to a principle which he deemed essential to liberty and justice. He loved his country as only a man in close touch with its history and with a deep reverence for its great founder, Washington, could love it; he had fought for its flag; he wore its uniform; he had been educated at its expense; and General Scott, the Commander of the army, a devoted Union man, was his warm personal friend. Patriotism, personal pride, loyalty and even gratitude, therefore, urged him toward the support of the Union, and only his adherence to a principle and the claims of his kinsmen and friends forbade.

For a time Virginia resisted every effort to induce her to cast her lot with the Confederacy. Indeed she actually voted against secession when the question was first presented. But when Fort Sumter resisted attack on April 12, 1861, and the President called upon the various states to furnish troops to enforce the national authority, practically all affection for the Union disappeared and by a decisive vote Virginia determined to uphold the Southern cause.

At that crisis President Lincoln made a strong effort to induce Lee to support the Union, for he actually offered him the command of the United States Army which was about to take the field. The full force of this remarkable tribute to his professional skill was not lost upon Lee. He had devoted his whole life to the army, and to be a successor of Washington in the command of that army meant more to him than perhaps to any other soldier in the land. Certainly, if he had consulted his own ambition or been influenced by any but the most unselfish motives, he would have accepted the call as the highest honor in the gift of the nation. But to do so he would have been obliged to surrender his private principles and desert his native state, and it is impossible to imagine that a man of his character would, even for an instant, consider such a course. Gravely and sadly he declined the mighty office, and two days later he tendered his resignation from the service he had honored for almost six and thirty years.

For this and his subsequent action Lee has been called a traitor and severely criticized for well-nigh fifty years. But, when a nation has been divided against itself upon a great issue of government, millions upon one side and millions upon the other, and half a century has intervened, it is high time that justice be given to the man who did what he thought right and honorably fought for a principle which he could have surrendered only at the expense of his conscience and his honor. Lee was a traitor to the United States in the same sense that Washington was a traitor to England. No more and no less. England takes pride to-day in having given

Washington to the world. Americans deprive their country of one of her claims to greatness when they fail to honor the character and the genius of Robert Lee.

It was in a letter to his old commander, Scott, that Lee announced his momentous decision, and its tone well indicated what the parting cost him.

"Arlington, Va., April 20, 1861.

"General:

"Since my interview with you on the 18th inst., I have felt that I ought not longer to retain my commission in the army. I, therefore, tender my resignation, which I request you will recommend for acceptance. It would have been presented at once but for the struggle it has cost me to separate myself from a service to which I have devoted the best years of my life and all the ability I possessed. During the whole of that time...I have experienced nothing but kindness from my superiors and a most cordial friendship from my comrades. To no one, General, have I been as much indebted as to yourself for uniform kindness and consideration.... Save in the defense of my native State, I never desire again to draw my sword."

Lee was fully aware of the serious nature of the conflict in which the country was about to engage. Americans were to be pitted against Americans and he knew what that meant. Wise men, both North and South, were prophesying that the war would not last more than ninety days, and foolish ones were bragging of their own powers and questioning the courage of their opponents, quite oblivious of the adage that when Greek meets Greek there comes a tug of war. But Lee did not concern himself with such childish exhibitions of judgment and temper.

"Do not put your faith in rumors of adjustment," he wrote his wife before serious fighting had begun. "I see no prospect of it. It cannot be while passions on both sides are so infuriated. MAKE YOUR PLANS FOR SEVERAL YEARS OF WAR. I agree with you that the inflammatory articles in the papers do us much harm. I object particularly to those in the Southern papers, as I wish them to take a firm, dignified course, free from bravado and boasting. The times are indeed calamitous. The brightness of God's countenance seems turned from us. It may not always be so dark and He may in time pardon our sins and take us under his protection."

Up to this time his son Custis, who had graduated first in his class at West Point, was still in the service of the United States as a lieutenant in the Engineers and of him Lee wrote to his wife in the same comradely spirit that he had always shown toward his boys. "Tell Custis he must consult his own judgment, reason and conscience, as to the course he may take. The present is a momentous question which every man must settle for himself, and upon principle. I do not wish him to be guided by my wishes or example. If I have done wrong let him do better."

Virginia was not slow in recognizing that she had within her borders the soldiers whom the chief general of the United States described as the greatest military genius in America, and within three days of his resignation from the old army, Lee was tendered the command of all the Virginia troops. Convinced that the brunt of the heavy fighting would fall on his native state, to whose defense he had dedicated his sword, he accepted the offer and thus there came to the aid of the Confederacy one of the few really great commanders that the world has ever seen.

Chapter XII
Opening Moves

It was to no very agreeable task that Lee was assigned at the outset of his command. The forces of the Confederacy were even less prepared to take the field than those of the United States, and for three months Lee was hard at work organizing and equipping the army for effective service. This important but dull duty prevented him from taking any active part in the first great battle of the War at Bull Run (July 21, 1861), but it was his rare judgment in massing the troops where they could readily reenforce each other that enabled the Confederate commanders on that occasion to form the junction which resulted in the overwhelming defeat of the Union army. This fact was well recognized by the authorities and, when the situation in western Virginia assumed a threatening aspect, he was ordered there with the highest hopes that he would repeat the success of Bull Run and speedily expel the Union forces from that part of the state.

A more unpromising field of operation than western Virginia could scarcely have been selected for the new commander. The people of that region generally favored the Union, and the Federal troops had already obtained possession of the strongest positions, while some of the Confederate commanders were quarreling with each other and otherwise working at cross purposes. For a time, therefore, Lee had to devote himself to smoothing over the differences which had arisen among his jealous subordinates, but when he at last began an aggressive movement, bad weather and a lack of cooperation between the various parts of his small army defeated his designs, and in October, 1861, the three-months' campaign came to an inglorious close.

This complete failure was a bitter disappointment to the Confederate hopes and Lee was severely blamed for the result. Indeed, for the time being he was regarded as an overrated individual who had had his opportunity and had proved unequal to the task of conducting military operations on a large scale. It was not easy to suffer this unjust criticism to pass unnoticed, but the discipline of the army life had taught Lee to control his tongue, and he made no protest even when he found himself removed from the front to superintend the fortifying of the coast. A small-minded man would probably have retired in sulky silence under such circumstances, but Lee entered upon his new duties with cheerful energy, and in four months he devised such skillful defenses for Charleston, Savannah and other points on the Confederate coast line, that they were enabled to defy all assaults of the Union army and navy until almost the close of the war. This invaluable service attracted no public attention, but it was fully appreciated by the Confederate authorities, who in no wise shared the popular opinion concerning Lee's talents. On the contrary, President Jefferson Davis, himself a graduate of West Point, continued to have the highest regard for his ability, and in March, 1862, he reappointed him as his chief military adviser at Richmond.

It was about this time that the roar of cannon in the West attracted the attention of the country, making it realize for the first time how far flung was the battle line of the contending armies; and on hard-fought fields, hundreds and hundreds of miles away from Washington and Richmond, the mud-splashed figure of Grant began to loom through heavy clouds of smoke.

It was by no brilliant achievement that Grant regained his standing in the army. The unruly 21st Illinois had been sufficiently disciplined within a fortnight after he assumed command to take some pride in itself as an organization and when its short term of service expired, it responded to the eloquence of McClernand and Logan, two visiting orators, by reenlisting almost to a man. Then the Colonel set to work in earnest to make his regiment ready for the field, drilling and hardening the men for their duties and waiting for an opportunity to show that this was a fighting force with no nonsense about it. The opportunity came sooner than he expected, for about two weeks after he had assumed command, his regiment was ordered to northern Missouri, and a railroad official called at his camp to inquire how many cars he would need for the transportation of his men. "I don't want any," was the bluff response; and, to the astonishment of the local authorities who, at that period of the war, never dreamed of moving troops except by rail or river, the energetic

Colonel assembled his regiment in marching order and started it at a brisk pace straight across country.

But, though he had moved with such commendable promptness, Grant was not nearly so confident as his actions seemed to imply. In fact, before he reached his destination, he heartily wished himself back again, and by the time he arrived at the point where the enemy was expected his nerves were completely unstrung. It was not the fright of cowardice that unmanned him, but rather the terror of responsibility. Again and again he had braved death in battle but now, for the first time, the safety of an entire regiment depended solely upon him as he approached the summit of the hill from which he expected to catch sight of his opponents he dreaded to fight them, lest he prove unequal to the emergency. But, while he was tormenting himself with this over-anxiety, he suddenly remembered that his opponent was just as new at his duties as he was and probably quite as nervous, and from that moment his confidence gradually returned. As a matter of fact, Colonel Harris, who commanded the Confederate force, displayed far more prudence than valor, for, on hearing of the advance of the Union troops, he speedily retreated and the 21st Illinois encountered no opposition whatever. But the march taught Grant a lesson he never forgot and, thereafter, in the hour of peril, he invariably consoled himself by remembering that his opponents were not free from danger and the more he made them look to their own safety the less time they would have for worrying him.

It was in July, 1861, when Grant entered Missouri, and about a month later the astonishing news reached his headquarters that President Lincoln had appointed him a Brigadier General of Volunteers. The explanation of this unexpected honor was that the Illinois Congressmen had included his name with seven others on a list of possible brigadiers, and the President had appointed four of them without further evidence of their qualifications. Under such circumstances, the promotion was not much of an honor, but it placed Grant in immediate command of an important district involving the control of an army of quite respectable size.

For a time the new General was exclusively occupied with perfecting the organization of his increased command, but to this hard, dull work he devoted himself in a manner that astonished some of the other brigadiers whose ideas of the position involved a showy staff of officers and a deal of picturesque posing in resplendent uniforms. But Grant had no patience with such foolery. He had work to do and when his headquarters were established at Cairo, Illinois, he took charge of them himself, keeping his eyes on all the details like any careful business man. In fact he was, as far as appearances were concerned, a man of business, for he seldom wore a uniform and worked at his desk all day in his shirt sleeves, behind ramparts of maps and papers, with no regard whatever for military ceremony or display.

A month of this arduous preparation found his force ready for active duty and about this time he became convinced that the Confederates intended to seize Paducah, an important position in Kentucky at the mouth of the Tennessee River, just beyond the limits of his command. He, accordingly, telegraphed his superiors for permission to occupy the place. No reply came to this request and a more timid man would have hesitated to move without orders. But Grant saw the danger and, assuming the responsibility, landed his troops in the town just in time to prevent its capture by the Confederates. Paducah was in sympathy with the South, and on entering it the Union commander issued an address to the inhabitants which attracted far more attention than the occupation of the town, for it contained nothing of the silly brag and bluster so common then in military proclamations on both sides. On the contrary, it was so modest and sensible, and yet so firm, that Lincoln, on reading it, is said to have remarked: "The man who can write like that is fitted to command."

Paducah was destined to be the last of Grant's bloodless victories, for in November, 1861, he was ordered to threaten the Confederates near Belmont, Missouri, as a feint to keep them from reenforcing another point where a real assault was planned. The maneuver was conducted with great energy and promised to be completely successful, but after Grant's raw troops had made their first onslaught and had driven their opponents from the field, they became disorderly and before he could control them the enemy reappeared in overwhelming numbers and compelled them to fight their way back to the river steamers which had carried them to the scene of action. This they succeeded in doing, but such was their haste to escape capture that they actually tumbled on board the boats and pushed off from the shore without waiting for their commander. By this time the Confederates were rapidly approaching with the intention of sweeping the decks of the crowded steamboats before they could get out of range, and Grant was apparently cut off from all chance of escape. Directly in front of him lay the precipitous river bank, while below only one transport was within hail and that had already started from its moorings. Its captain, however, caught sight of him as he came galloping through a corn field and instantly pushed his vessel as close to the shore as he dared, at the same time throwing out a single plank about fifteen feet in length to serve as an emergency gangway. To force a horse down the cliff-like bank of the river and up the narrow plank to the steamer's deck, was a daring feat, but the officer who was riding for his life had not forgotten the skill which had marked him at West Point and, compelling his mount to slide on its haunches down the slippery mud precipice, he trotted coolly up the dangerous incline to safety.

The battle of Belmont (November 7, 1861), as this baptism of fire was called, is said to have caused more mourning than almost any other engagement of the war, for up to that time there had been but little loss of life and its list of killed and wounded, mounting into the hundreds, made a painfully deep impression. In this respect, it was decidedly ominous of Grant's future record, but it accomplished his purpose in detaining the Confederates and he was soon to prove his willingness to accept defeats as necessary incidents to any successful campaign and to fight on undismayed.

Chapter XIII
Grant's First Success

Up to this time the war in the West had been largely an affair of skirmishes. A body of Union troops would find itself confronting a Confederate force, one of the two commanders would attack and a fight would follow; or the Confederates would march into a town and their opponents would attempt to drive them out of it, not because it was of any particular value, but because the other side held it. "See-a-head-and-hit-it" strategy governed the day and no plan worthy of the name had been adopted for conducting the war on scientific principles.

But Grant had studied the maps to some purpose in his office at Cairo and he realized that the possession of the Mississippi River was the key to the situation in the West. As long as the Confederates controlled that great waterway which afforded them free access to the ocean and fairly divided the Eastern from the Western States, they might reasonably hope to defy their opponents to the end of time. But, if they lost it, one part of the Confederacy would be almost completely cut off from the rest. Doubtless, other men saw this just as clearly and quite as soon as Grant did; but having once grasped an idea he never lost sight of it, and while others were diverted by minor matters, he concentrated his whole attention on what he believed to be the vital object of all campaigning in the West.

The Tennessee River and the Cumberland River both flow into the Ohio, not far from where that river empties into the Mississippi. They, therefore, formed the principal means of water communication with the Mississippi for the State of Tennessee, and the Confederates had created forts to protect them at points well within supporting distance of each other. Fort Henry, guarding the Tennessee River, and Fort Donelson, commanding the Cumberland River, were both in Grant's district, and in January, 1862, he wrote to General Halleck, his superior officer in St. Louis, calling attention to the importance of these posts and offering suggestions for their capture. But Halleck did not take any notice of this communication and Grant thereupon resolved to go to St. Louis and present his plans in person. This was the first time he had been in the city since the great change in his circumstances and those who had known him only a few years before as a poverty-stricken farmer and wagoner could scarcely believe that he was the same man. He had, as yet, done nothing very remarkable, but he held an important command, his name was well and favorably known and he had already begun to pay off his old debts. All this enabled his father and mother to regain something of the pride they had once felt for their eldest son, and his former friends were glad to welcome him and claim his acquaintance.

Pleasant as this was, the trip to St. Louis was a bitter disappointment in other respects, for Halleck not only rejected his subordinate's proposition for the capture of Fort Henry and Fort Donelson, but dismissed him without even listening to the details of his plan. Most officers would have been completely discouraged by such treatment, but Grant had been accustomed to disappointments for many years and did not readily despair. Meeting Flag-Officer Foote who had charge of a fleet of gun boats near Cairo, he explained his idea and finding him not only sympathetic, but enthusiastic, he and Foote each sent a telegram to Halleck assuring him that Fort Henry could be taken if he would only give his consent. These messages brought no immediate response, but Grant continued to request permission to advance until, on the 1st of February, 1862, the necessary order was obtained and within twenty-four hours the persistent officer had his expedition well upon its way.

His force consisted of some 15,000 men and seven gun boats, and Halleck promised him reenforcements, sending a capable officer to see that they were promptly forwarded. This officer was Brigadier General Sherman who thus, for the first time, came in touch with the man with whom he was destined to bring the war to a close. Four days after the troops started they were ready to attack and the gun-boats at once proceeded to shell the fort, with the result that its garrison almost immediately surrendered (February 6, 1862), practically all of its defenders having retreated to Fort Donelson as soon as they saw that their position was seriously threatened.

Grant promptly notified his Chief of this easy conquest, at the same time adding that he would take Fort Donelson within forty-eight hours, but he soon had reason to regret this boast--one of the few of which he was ever guilty. Indeed, his troops had scarcely started on their journey when rapid progress became impossible, for the rain descended in torrents, rendering the roads impassable for wagons and cannon, and almost impracticable for infantry or cavalry. Moreover, many of the men had foolishly thrown away their blankets and overcoats during the march from Fort Henry and their suffering under the freezing winter blasts was exceedingly severe, especially as camp fires were not permitted for fear that their smoke would attract the gunners in the fort. Under these circumstances the advance was seriously delayed, and it was February 14, 1862--six days after he had prophesied that he would take the place--before Grant had his army in position. By this time, however, the gun-boats had arrived and he determined to attack at once, although Halleck had advised him to wait for reenforcements to occupy Fort Henry, lest the Confederates should recapture it while his back was turned. There was, of course, a chance of this, but Grant felt sure that if he delayed the Confederates would seize the opportunity to strengthen Fort Donelson, and then 50,000 men would not be able to accomplish what 15,000 might immediately effect. He, accordingly, directed Foote to bombard the fort at once from the river front and try to run its batteries. Desperate as this attempt appeared his orders were instantly obeyed, the fearless naval officer forcing his little vessels into the very jaws of death under a terrific fire, to which he responded with a hail of shot and shell.

Grant watched this spectacular combat with intense interest, waiting for a favorable moment to order an advance of his troops, but to his bitter disappointment one after another of Foote's vessels succumbed to the deadly fire of the water batteries and drifted helplessly back with the current. Indeed, the flagship was struck more than sixty times and Foote himself was so severely wounded that he could not report in person, but requested that the General come on board his ship for a conference, which disclosed the fact that the fleet was in no condition to continue the combat and must retire for repairs.

There was nothing for Grant to do, therefore, but prepare for a siege, and with a heavy heart he returned from the battered gun-boat to give the necessary orders. He had scarcely set his foot on shore, however, before a staff officer dashed up with the startling intelligence that the Confederates had sallied forth and attacked a division of the army commanded by General McClernand and that his troops were fleeing in a panic which threatened to involve the entire army. Grant knew McClernand well. He was one of the Congressmen who had made speeches to the 21st Illinois and, realizing that the man was almost wholly ignorant of military matters and utterly incapable of handling such a situation, he leaped on his horse and, spurring his way across the frozen ground to the sound of the firing, confronted the huddled and beaten division just in the nick of time. Meanwhile, General Lew Wallace--afterwards famous as the author "Ben Hur"--had arrived and thrown forward a brigade to cover the confused retreat, so that for the moment the Confederate advance was held in check. But despite this, McClernand's men continued to give way, muttering that their ammunition was exhausted. There were tons of ammunition close at hand, as the officers ought to have known had they understood their duties, but even when assured of this the panic-stricken soldiers refused to return to the field. They were in no condition to resist attack, they declared, and the enemy was evidently intending to make a long fight of it, as the haversacks of those who had fallen contained at least three days' rations. This excuse was overheard by Grant and instantly riveted his attention.

"Let me see some of those haversacks," he commanded sharply, and one glance at their contents convinced him that the Confederates were not attempting to crush his army, but were trying to break through his lines and escape. If they intended to stay and defend the fortress, they would not carry haversacks at all; but if they contemplated a retreat, they would not only take them, but fill them with enough provisions to last for several days. In reaching this conclusion Grant was greatly aided by his knowledge of the men opposing him. He had served in Mexico with General Pillow, the second in command at Fort Donelson, and, knowing him to be a timid man, felt certain that nothing but desperation would ever induce him to risk an attack. He also knew that Floyd, his immediate superior, who had recently been the United States Secretary of War, had excellent reasons for avoiding capture and, putting all these facts together, he instantly rose to the occasion.

"Fill your cartridge boxes, quick, and get into line," was his order to the men as he dashed down the wavering lines. "The enemy is trying to escape and he must not be permitted to do so!"

The word flew through the disordered ranks, transforming them as it passed, and at the same time orders were issued for the entire left wing to advance and attack without a moment's delay. This unexpected onslaught quickly threw the Confederates back into the fortress, but before they again reached the shelter of its walls the Union forces had carried all the outer defenses and had virtually locked the door behind their retreating adversaries.

From that moment the capture of the imprisoned garrison was only a question of time, and within twenty-four hours Grant received a communication from the Confederate commander asking for a truce to consider the terms of surrender. To his utter astonishment, however, this suggestion did not come from either General Floyd or General Pillow but from Simon Buckner, his old friend at West Point, who had so generously aided him when he reached New York, penniless and disgraced after his resignation from the army. This was an embarrassing situation, indeed, but while he would have done anything he could for Buckner personally, Grant realized that he must not allow gratitude or friendship to interfere with his duty. He, therefore, promptly answered the proposal for a truce in these words:

"No terms except an unconditional and immediate surrender can be accepted. I propose to move immediately upon your works."

[NOTE from Brett: The full letter is also shown in Grant's handwriting which leaves something to be desired. I will do my best to transcribe it below:

Hd Qrs. Army in the Field Camp Fort Donelson, Feb. 16th 1862

Cmdr. S. B. Buckner Confed. Army.

Sir,

Yours of this inst. proposing armistice, and appointment of Commissioners to settle terms of Capitulation is just received. No terms except an unconditional and immediate surrender can be accepted.

I propose to move immediately upon your works.

I am Sir, very respectfully, your obt. svt. [obedient servant], U. S. Grant Brig. Gen.

A portion of this letter is found at http/www.livinghistoryonline.com/surrendr.htm]

But no more fighting was necessary, for Buckner yielded as gracefully as he could, and on February 16, 1862, he and the entire garrison of about 15,000 men became prisoners of war. Generals Pillow and Floyd, it appeared, had fled with some 4,000 men the night before, leaving Buckner in charge and as Grant's force had by that time been increased to 27,000 men, further resistance would have been useless.

The capture of these two forts gave the Union forces command of the Tennessee and the Cumberland Rivers, and to that extent cleared the way for the control of the Mississippi. It was the first real success which had greeted the Union cause and it raised Grant to a Major-Generalship of Volunteers, gave him a national reputation and supplied a better interpretation of his initial than West Point had provided, for from the date of his letter to Buckner he was known as "Unconditional Surrender" Grant.

Chapter XIV
The Battle of Shiloh

Grant did not waste any time in rejoicing over his success. The capture of Fort Henry and Fort Donelson was an important achievement but it was only one step toward the control of the Mississippi River, which was the main object of the campaign. The next step in that direction was toward Corinth a strategically important point in Mississippi, and he immediately concentrated his attention upon getting the army in position to attack that stronghold. Some of his fellow commanders, however, were extremely cautious and he had to labor for days before he could persuade General Buell, who was stationed at Nashville, Tennessee, with a large army, to advance his troops to a point where they could be of service. But in the midst of this work he was suddenly interrupted by an order which removed him from his command and virtually placed him under arrest on charges of disregarding instructions and of being absent from his department without permission.

These astonishing accusations were caused by his failure to answer dispatches from Headquarters which had never reached him, and by his visit to General Buell which had obliged him to travel beyond the strict limits of his command. The whole matter was soon explained by the discovery that a Confederate had been tampering with the dispatches in the telegraph office, but it was exceedingly annoying to Grant to find himself publicly condemned without a hearing. Nevertheless, it supplied a very fair test of his character, for he neither lost his temper nor displayed any excitement whatsoever. On the contrary, he remained perfectly calm in the face of grave provocation, replying firmly but respectfully to the harsh criticisms of his superiors, and behaving generally with a dignity and composure that won the silent approval of all observers.

Of course, as soon as the facts were known he was restored to his command with an ample apology, but his preparations for the advance against Corinth had been seriously interrupted and it was some time before he again had the work in hand. Nevertheless, within five weeks of the surrender of Fort Donelson, he was headed toward Mississippi with over 30,000 men, having arranged with General Buell to follow and support him with his army of 40,000, the combined forces being amply sufficient to overpower the Confederates who were guarding Corinth. This vast superiority, however, probably served to put Grant off his guard, for on March 16, 1862, his advance under General Sherman reached Pittsburg Landing, not far from Corinth, and encamped there without taking the precaution to intrench. Sherman reported on April 5th that he had no fear of being attacked and Grant, who had been injured the day before by the fall of his horse and was still on crutches, remained some distance in the rear, feeling confident that there would be no serious fighting for several days.

But the Union commander, who had studied his opponents with such good results at Fort Donelson, made a terrible mistake in failing to do so on this occasion, for he knew, or ought to have known, that General Albert Sidney Johnston and General Beauregard, the Confederate commanders were bold and energetic officers who were well advised of the military situation and ready to take advantage of every opportunity. Indeed, their sharp eyes had already noted the gap between Grant's and Buell's armies and at the moment Sherman was penning his dispatch to his superior, informing him that all was well, a force of 40,000 men was preparing to crush his unprotected advance guard before Buell could reach the field.

It was Sunday morning, April 6, 1862, when the ominous sound of firing in the direction of Shiloh Church smote Grant's ears. For a few moments he could not believe that it indicated a serious attack, but the roar of heavy guns soon convinced him that a desperate battle had begun and, directing his orderlies to lift him into the saddle, he dashed to the nearest boat landing and proceeded to the front with all possible speed. Before he reached the ground, however, the Confederates had driven the Union outposts from the field in frightful disorder and were hurling themselves with ferocious energy upon those who still held fast. The surprise had been well-nigh complete and the first rush of the gray infantry carried everything before it, leaving the foremost Union camp in their hands. Indeed, for a time the

Federal army was not much more than a disorganized mob, completely bewildered by the shock of battle, and thousands of men blindly sought refuge in the rear, heedless of their officers who, with a few exceptions, strove valiantly to organize an effective defense.

The tumult and confusion were at their worst when Grant reached the field and it seemed almost hopeless to check the panic and prevent the destruction of his entire army. But in the midst of the maddening turmoil and wild scenes of disaster he kept his head and, dashing from one end of the line to the other, ordered regiments into position with a force and energy that compelled obedience. There was no time to formulate any plan of battle. Each officer had to do whatever he thought best to hold back the Confederates in his immediate front, and for hours the fight was conducted practically without orders. But Grant supplied his gallant subordinates with something far more important than orders at that crisis. Undismayed by the chaos about him he remained cool and inspired them with confidence. Not for one instant would he admit the possibility of defeat, and under his strong hand the huddled lines were quickly reformed, the onrush of the Confederates was gradually checked and a desperate conflict begun for every inch of ground.

For a time the victorious gray-coats continued to push their opponents back and another line of tents fell into their hands. But their advance was stubbornly contested and knowing that Buell was at hand, Grant fought hard for delay, using every effort to encourage his men to stand fast and present the boldest possible front to the foe. Meanwhile, however, Sherman was wounded, and when darkness put an end to the furious combat the shattered Union army was on the verge of collapse. So perilous, indeed, was the situation that when Buell arrived on the field his first inquiry was as to what preparations Grant had made to effect a retreat. But the silent commander instantly shook his head and announced, to the intense astonishment of his questioner, that he did not intend to retreat but to attack at daylight the next morning with every man at his disposal, leaving no reserves.

Such was Grant at one of the darkest moments of his career. Behind him lay the battered remnants of regiments, screening a welter of confusion and fear; before him stretched the blood-soaked field of Shiloh held by the confident Confederate host; while at his elbow stood anxious officers, well satisfied to have saved the army from destruction and ready to point out a convenient line of retreat. All his surroundings, in fact, were calculated to discourage him and the intense pain of his injured leg, which allowed him neither rest nor sleep, was a severe strain upon his nerves. Yet he would not yield to weakness of any kind. He was responsible for the position in which the Union army found itself and he determined to retrieve its fortunes. Therefore, all night long while reenforcements were steadily arriving, he developed his plans for assuming the offensive, and at break of day his troops hurled themselves against the opposing lines with dauntless energy.

Meanwhile the Confederates had sustained an irreparable loss, for Albert Sidney Johnston, their brilliant leader, had fallen. Moreover, they had no reserves to meet the Union reenforcements. Nevertheless, they received the vigorous onslaught with splendid courage and another terrible day of carnage followed. Again and again Grant exposed himself with reckless daring, narrowly escaping death from a bullet which carried away the scabbard of his sword as he reconnoitered in advance of his men, but despite his utmost efforts the gray lines held fast, and for hours no apparent advantage was gained. Then, little by little, the heavy Union battalions began to push them back until all the lost ground was recovered, but the Confederates conducted their retreat in good order and finally reached a point of safety, leaving very few prisoners in their pursuers' hands.

Grant had saved his army from destruction and had even driven his adversary from the field, but at a fearful cost, for no less than 10,000 Union soldiers were killed or wounded in the two days' desperate fighting at Shiloh and almost 3,000 had been captured. The Confederates, it is true, had lost nearly 10,000 men, but their army, which should have been crushed by the combined efforts of Grant and Buell, was still in possession of Corinth and had come dangerously near to annihilating half of the Union forces.

The results of the battle were, therefore, received at Washington with surprise and indignation; the country at large, horrified at the frightful slaughter, denounced it as a useless butchery; Halleck hastily assumed charge of all the forces in the field and from that time forward Grant, though nominally the second in command, was deprived of all power and virtually reduced to the role of a mere spectator. Indeed, serious efforts were made to have him dismissed from the service, but Lincoln after carefully considering the charges, refused to act. "I can't spare this man," was his comment. "He FIGHTS."

Lincoln intended to imply by that remark that there were generals in the army who did not fight, and Halleck was certainly one of them, for he took thirty-one days to march the distance that the Confederates had covered in three. Indeed, he displayed such extraordinary caution that with an army of 100,000 at his back he inched his way toward Corinth, erecting intrenchments at every halt, only to find, after a month, that he had been frightened by shadows and dummy guns and that the city had been abandoned by the Confederates. No commander responsible for such a ridiculous performance could retain the confidence of an army in the field, and Sherman assured Grant that Halleck would not long survive the fiasco. This advice was sorely needed, for Grant had grown tired of being constantly humiliated and had already requested Halleck to relieve him from duty when Sherman persuaded him to remain and wait for something to happen.

Something happened sooner then either man expected, for Halleck was suddenly "kicked up stairs" by his appointment to the chief command with headquarters in Washington, and on July 11, 1862, about three months after the battle of Shiloh, Grant found himself again at the head of a powerful army.

Chapter XV
Lee in the Saddle

While Grant was earning a reputation as a fighting general in the West, Lee had been at a desk in Richmond attending to his duties as chief military adviser to the Confederate President, which prevented him from taking active part in any operations in the field. As a matter of fact, however, there had been no important engagements in the East, for "On to Richmond!" had become the war cry of the North, and all the energies of the Federal government had been centered on preparations for the capture of the Southern capital. Indeed, if Richmond had been the treasure house and last refuge of the Confederacy, no greater efforts could have been made to secure it, although it was by no means essential to either the North or the South and the war would have continued no matter which flag floated above its roofs. Nevertheless, the idea of marching into the enemy's capital appealed to the popular imagination and this undoubtedly dictated much of the early strategy of the war.

At all events, while the opening moves in the campaign for the possession of the Mississippi were being made, a vast army was being equipped near Washington for the express purpose of capturing Richmond. The preparation of this force had been entrusted to General George B. McClellan whose ability in organizing, drilling and disciplining the troops had made him a popular hero and given him such a reputation as a military genius that he was universally hailed as "the young Napoleon." He had, indeed, created the most thoroughly equipped army ever seen in America, and when he advanced toward Virginia in April, 1862, at the head of over 100,000 men the supporters of the Union believed that the doom of the Confederacy was already sealed.

From this office in Richmond Lee watched these formidable preparations for invading the South with no little apprehension. He knew that the Confederates had only about 50,000 available troops with which to oppose McClellan's great army and had the Union commander been aware of this he might have moved straight against the city and swept its defenders from his path. But McClellan always believed that he was outnumbered and on this occasion he wildly exaggerated his opponents' strength. In fact, he crept forward so cautiously that the Confederates, who had almost resigned themselves to losing the city, hastened to bring up reenforcements and erect defensive works of a really formidable character. The best that was hoped for, however, was to delay the Union army. To defeat it, or even to check its advance, seemed impossible, and doubtless it would have proved so had it not been for the brilliant exploits of the man who was destined to become Lee's "right hand."

This man was General Thomas Jonathan Jackson, who had earned the nickname of "Stonewall" at Bull Run and was at that time in command of about 15,000 men guarding the fertile Shenandoah Valley, the "granary of Virginia." Opposing this comparatively small army were several strong Union forces which were considered amply sufficient to capture or destroy it, and McClellan proceeded southward, with no misgivings concerning Jackson. But the wily Confederate had no intention of remaining idle and McClellan's back was scarcely turned before he attacked and utterly routed his nearest opponents. A second, third and even a fourth army was launched against him, but he twisted, turned and doubled on his tracks with bewildering rapidity, cleverly luring his opponents apart; and then, falling on each in turn with overwhelming numbers, hurled them from his path with astonishing ease and suddenly appeared before Washington threatening its capture.

Astounded and alarmed at this unexpected peril, the Federal authorities instantly ordered McDowell's corps of 40,000 men, which was on the point of joining McClellan, to remain and defend the capital. This was a serious blow to McClellan who had counted upon using these troops, though even without them he greatly outnumbered the Confederates. But the idea that he was opposed by an overwhelming force had taken such a firm hold on his mind that he was almost afraid to move, and while he was timidly feeling his way General Joseph Johnston, commanding the defenses at Richmond, attacked his advance corps at Seven Pines, May 31, 1862. A fierce contest followed, during which Johnston was severely wounded, and Jefferson Davis, who was on the field, promptly summoned General Lee to the command.

It was a serious situation which confronted Lee when he was thus suddenly re-called to active duty, for McClellan's army outnumbered his by at least 40,000 men and it was within six miles of Richmond, from the roofs of whose houses the glow of the Union campfires was plainly visible. Nevertheless, he determined to put on a bold front and attack his opponent at his weakest point. But how to discover this was a difficult problem and the situation did not admit of a moment's delay. Under ordinary circumstances the information might have been secured through spies, but there was no time for this and confronted by the necessity for immediate action, Lee thought of "Jeb" Stuart, his son's classmate at West Point, who had acted as aide in the capture of John Brown.

Stuart was only twenty-nine years old but he had already made a name for himself as a general of cavalry, and Lee knew him well enough to feel confident that, if there was any one in the army who could procure the needed information, he was the man. He, accordingly, ordered him to take 1,200 troopers and a few field guns and ride straight at the right flank of the Union army until he got near enough to learn how McClellan's forces were posted at that point.

This perilous errand was just the opportunity for which Stuart had been wait-ing, and without the loss of a moment he set his horsemen in motion. Directly in his path lay the Federal cavalry but within twenty-four hours he had forced his way through them and carefully noted the exact position of the Union troops. His mission was then accomplished, but by this time the Federal camp was thoroughly aroused and, knowing that if he attempted to retrace his steps his capture was al-most certain, he pushed rapidly forward and, passing around the right wing, pro-ceeded to circle the rear of McClellan's entire army. So speedily did he move that the alarm of his approach was no sooner given in one quarter than he appeared in another and thus, like a boy disturbing a row of hornets' nests with a long stick, he flashed by the whole line, reached the Union left, swung around it and reported to Lee with his command practically intact.

That a few squadrons of cavalry should have been able to ride around his army of 100,000 men and escape unscathed astonished and annoyed McClellan but he utterly failed to grasp the true purpose of this brilliant exploit, and Lee took the utmost care to see that his suspicions were not aroused. Stuart's information had convinced him that the right wing of the Union army was badly exposed and might be attacked with every prospect of success, but to insure this it was necessary that McClellan's attention should be distracted from the real point of danger. The Confederate commander thoroughly understood his opponent's character and failings, for he had taken his measure during the Mexican War and knowing his cautious nature, he spread the news that heavy reenforcements had been forwarded to Jackson in the Shenandoah Valley. This he felt sure would confirm McClellan's belief that he had such overwhelming numbers that he could afford to withdraw troops from Richmond, and the ruse was entirely successful, for the Union commander hesitated to advance, and the Federal authorities, hearing of Jackson's supposed reenforcement, became increasingly alarmed for the safety of Washington.

Meanwhile, a courier had been secretly hurried to Jackson, ordering him to rush his troops from the Shenandoah Valley and attack McClellan's right wing from the rear while Lee assaulted it from the front. But the Union right wing numbered fully 25,000 men and Jackson had only 15,000. So to make the attack overwhelming it was necessary for Lee to withdraw 40,000 men from the defenses of Richmond, leaving the city practically unprotected. Unquestionably, this was a most dangerous move, for had McClellan suspected the truth he might have forced his way into the capital without much difficulty. But here again Lee counted upon his adversary's character, for he directed the troops that remained in the trenches to keep up a continuous feint of attacking the Union left wing, in the hope that this show of force would cause McClellan to look to his safety in that quarter, which is precisely what he did. Indeed, he was still busy reporting the threatening movements against his left, when Lee and Jackson's combined force of 55,000 men fell upon his right with fearful effect at Gaines' Mill (June 27, 1862). From that moment his campaign for the capture of Richmond became a struggle to save his own army from capture or destruction.

The only safety lay in flight but at the moment of defeat and impending disaster it was not easy to extricate the troops from their dangerous position, and McClellan showed high skill in masking his line of retreat. Lee did not, therefore, immediately discover the direction in which he was moving and this delay probably prevented him from annihilating the remnants of the Union army. Once on the trail, however, he lost no time and, loosing "his dogs of war," they fell upon the retreating columns again and again in the series of terrible conflicts known as the "Seven Days' Battles." But the Union army was struggling for its life and, like a stag at bay, it fought off its pursuers with desperate courage, until finally at Malvern Hill (July 1, 1862), it rolled them back with such slaughter that a bolder leader might have been encouraged to advance again toward Richmond. As it was, however, McClellan was well content to remove his shattered legions to a point of safety at Harrison's Landing, leaving Lee in undisturbed possession of the field dyed with the blood of well-nigh 30,000 men.

Chapter XVI
A Game of Strategy

While the remnants of McClellan's fine army were recuperating from the rough handling they had received, Lee was developing a plan to remove them still further from the vicinity of Richmond. Harrison's Landing was too close to the Confederate capital for comfort and the breastworks which the Union commander erected there were too formidable to be attacked. But, though he could not hope to drive his adversary away by force, Lee believed that he could lure him from his stronghold by carrying the war into another part of Virginia. The opportunity to do this was particularly favorable, for the Union forces in front of Washington, consisting of about 45,000 men, had been placed under the command of General John Pope. Pope had served with Grant in the Mississippi campaign and had begun his career in the East by boasting of the great things he was about to accomplish, referring contemptuously to his opponents and otherwise advertising himself as a braggart and a babbler. He had come, so he told his soldiers in a flamboyant address, from an army which had seen only the backs of its enemies. He had come to lead them to victories. He wanted to hear no more of "lines of retreat" or backward movements of any kind. His headquarters were "in the saddle" and his mission was to terrorize the foe.

These absurd proclamations pretty thoroughly exposed Pope's character, but he had been at West Point with General Longstreet, one of Lee's ablest advisers, and that officer speedily acquainted his chief with the full measure of his opponent's weaknesses. This was exceedingly useful to Lee and when he discovered that McClellan and Pope were pulling at different directions like balky circus horses, while Halleck with one foot on each was in imminent peril of a fall, he determined to take advantage of the situation and hasten the disaster.

McClellan, having 90,000 men, wanted Pope to reenforce him with his 45,000, and thus insure a renewal of his campaign against Richmond. But this, of course, did not suit Pope who wished McClellan's army to reenforce him and march to victory under his banner. But while each of the rivals was insisting that his plan should be adopted and Halleck, who held the chief of command, was wobbling between them, trying to make up his mind to favor one or the other, Lee took the whole matter out of his hands and decided it for him. He did not want McClellan to be reenforced; first, because he was the abler officer and, second, because he had or soon would have more than sufficient men to capture Richmond and might wake to a realization of this fact at any moment. From the Confederate standpoint it was much safer to have Pope reenforced, for he did not have the experience necessary to handle a large army. Therefore, the more troops he had to mismanage the better. Moreover, Lee knew that McClellan would cease to be dangerous as soon as he was obliged to send any part of his forces away, for, as usual, he imagined that his opponents already outnumbered him and that the withdrawal of even a single regiment would place him practically at their mercy.

Carefully bearing all these facts in mind and thinking that it was about time to force Halleck to transfer some of McClellan's troops to Pope, Lee ordered Jackson to attack the man who thus far had seen "only the backs of his foes." But at the Battle of Cedar Mountain, which followed (August 9, 1862), his enemies would not turn their backs and the fact evidently alarmed him, for he immediately began shouting lustily for help. Perhaps he called a little louder than was necessary in order to get as many of his rival's men as possible under his own command, but the result was that McClellan's army began rapidly melting away under orders to hurry to the rescue.

Lee's first object was, therefore, accomplished at one stroke and, as fast as McClellan's troops moved northward, he withdrew the forces guarding Richmond and rushed them by shorter routes to confront Pope, whom he had determined to destroy before his reenforcements reached the field. Indeed, a very neat trap had already been prepared for that gentleman who was on the point of stepping into it when he intercepted one of his adversary's letters which gave him sufficient warning to escape by beating a hasty retreat across the Rappahannock River. This was a perfectly proper movement under the circumstances, but in view of his absurd ideas concerning retreats it opened him up to public ridicule which was almost more than a man of his character could endure. He was soon busy, therefore, complaining, explaining, and protesting his readiness to recross the river at a moment's notice.

But, while he was thus foolishly wearing out the telegraph lines between his headquarters and Washington, Lee was putting into operation a plan which would have been rash to the point of folly against a really able soldier but which was perfectly justified against an incompetent. This plan was to divide his army, which numbered less than 50,000 men, into two parts, sending "Stonewall" Jackson with 25,000 to get behind the Union forces, while he attracted their commander's attention at the front. Of course, if Pope had discovered this audacious move, he could easily have crushed the divided Confederate forces in turn before either could have come to the other's rescue, for he had 70,000 at his command. But the armies were not far from Manassas or Bull Run, where the first important engagement of the war had been fought and Lee know every inch of the ground. Moreover, he believed that all Pope's provisions and supplies upon which he depended for feeding his army were behind him, and that, if Jackson succeeded in seizing them and getting between the Union army and Washington, Pope would lose his head and dash to the rescue regardless of consequences.

Great, therefore, as the risk was he determined to take it, and Jackson circled away with his 25,000 men, leaving Lee with the same number confronting an army of 70,000 which might have swept the field. But its commander never dreamed of the opportunity which lay before him and he remained utterly unsuspicious until the night of August 26, 1862, when his flow of telegrams was suddenly checked and he was informed that there was something the matter with the wires connecting him to Washington. There was, indeed, something the matter with them, for Jackson's men had cut them down and were at that moment greedily devouring Pope's provisions, helping themselves to new uniforms and shoes and leaving facetious letters complaining of the quality of the supplies.

For a while, however, the Union general had no suspicion of what was happening, for he interpreted the interference with the telegraph wires as the work of cavalry riders whom a comparatively small force could quickly disperse. But when the troops dispatched for this purpose came hurrying back with the news that Jackson's whole army was behind them, he acted precisely as Lee had expected, and completely forgetting to close the doors behind him, dashed madly after "Stonewall," whom he regarded as safe as a cat in a bag.

The door which he should have closed was Thoroughfare Gap, for that was the only opening through which Lee could have led his men with any hope of arriving in time to help his friends, and a few troops could have blocked it with the utmost ease. But it was left unguarded and Pope had scarcely turned his back to spring on Jackson before Lee slid through the Gap and sprang on him.

The contest that followed, called the Second Battle of Bull Run or Manassas (August 30, 1862), was almost a repetition of the first, except that in the earlier battle the Union soldiers had a fair chance and on this occasion they had none at all. Indeed, Lee and Jackson had Pope so situated that, despite the bravery of his men, they battered and pounded him until he staggered from the field in a state of hysterical confusion, wildly telegraphing that the enemy was badly crippled and that everything would be well, and following up this by asking if the capital would be safe, if his army should be destroyed. It is indeed possible that his army would have been reduced to a mere mob, had it not been for the proximity of the fortifications of Washington, into which his exhausted regiments were safely tumbled on the 2nd of September, 1862.

Thus, for the second time in two months, Lee calmly confronted the wreck of an opposing host, which, at the outset, had outnumbered him and confidently planned for his destruction.

Chapter XVII
Lee and the Invasion of Maryland

L ee's masterly defense of Richmond, and his complete triumph over McClellan and Pope had, in three months, made him the idol of the Confederacy. In all military matters his word was law, while the army adored him and the people of the South as a whole regarded him with a feeling akin to reverence. This was not entirely the result of his achievements on the field. Jackson had displayed an equal genius for the art of war and in the opinion of many experts he was entitled to more credit than his chief. But Jackson was regarded with awe and curiosity rather than affection. He was hailed as a great commander, while Lee was recognized as a great man.

It was not by spectacular efforts or assertiveness of any kind that Lee had gained this hold upon his countrymen. He avoided everything that even tended toward self-display. His army reports were not only models of modesty, but generous acknowledgements of all he owed to his officers and men. He addressed none but respectful words to his superiors and indulged in no criticisms or complaints. He accepted the entire responsibility for whatever reverses occurred to the forces under his command and never attempted to place the blame on the shoulders of any other man. In a word, he was so absolutely free from personal ambition that the political schemers unconsciously stood abashed in his presence, and citizens and soldiers alike instinctively saluted the mere mention of his name.

Never by any chance did he utter a word of abuse against the North. Even when his beloved Arlington was seized, and the swords, pictures, silverware and other precious mementos of Washington were carried off, his protest was couched in quiet and dignified language, well calculated to make those to whom it was addressed (and later every American) blush with shame. Likewise in the heat of battle, when wild tongues were loosed and each side accused the other of all that hate could suggest, he never forgot that his opponents were Americans. "Drive those people back," or "Don't let those people pass you," were the harshest words he ever uttered of his foes.

To him war was not a mere license to destroy human life. It was a terrible weapon to be used scientifically, not with the idea of slaughtering as many of the enemy as possible, but to protect the State for whose defense he had drawn his sword. This was distinctly his attitude as he watched Pope's defeated columns reeling from the field. Neither by word nor deed did he exult over the fallen foe or indulge in self-glorification at his expense. His sole thought was to utilize the victory that the war would be speedily brought to a successful close; and, spreading out his maps in the quiet of his tent, he proceeded to study them with this idea.

Almost directly in front of his victorious army stretched the intrenchments of Washington but, although he knew something of the panic into which that city had been thrown by the last battle, he had not troops enough to risk assaulting fortifications to the defense of which well-nigh every able-bodied man in the vicinity had been called. The fall of Washington might perhaps have ended the war, but the loss of the neighboring state of Maryland and an attack on some of the Pennsylvania cities, such as Harrisburg and Philadelphia, promised to prove equally effective. The chances of wresting Maryland from the Union seemed particularly favorable, for it had come very close to casting its lot with the Confederacy and thousands of its citizens were serving in the Southern ranks. He, accordingly, made up his mind to march through Maryland, arousing its people to the support of the Confederate cause, and then carry the war into Pennsylvania where a decisive victory might pave the way to an acknowledgment of the independence of the Southern States and satisfactory terms of peace.

Thus, four days after Pope's defeat at Manassas saw Lee's tattered battle flags slanted toward the North, and on September 6, 1862, the vanguard under "Stonewall" Jackson passed through the streets of Frederick City, singing "Maryland, My Maryland!" This was the moment which Whittier immortalized in his verses recording the dramatic meeting between "Stonewall" and Barbara Frietchie [Note from Brett: The poem is entitled "Barbara Frietchie" and there is some question as to the accuracy of the details of the poem. In general, however, Whittier retold the story (poetically) that he claims he heard ("from respectable and trustworthy sources") and Barbara Frietchie was strongly against the Confederacy and was not a fictional character. It is believed that Ms. Frietchie, who was 95 at the time, was sick in bed on the day the soldiers marched through, but did wave her flag when the Union army marched through two days later. A Ms. Quantrill and her daughters, however, did wave the Union flag as the Confederate soldiers marched through the town, so there is some thought that the two got combined.]; but, though no such event ever took place, the poet was correctly informed as to the condition of Jackson's men, for they certainly were a "famished rebel horde." Indeed, several thousand of them had to be left behind because they could no longer march in their bare feet, and those who had shoes were sorry-looking scarecrows whose one square meal had been obtained at Pope's expense. For all practical purposes Maryland was the enemy's country, but into this hostile region they advanced carrying very little in the way of provisions except salt for the ears of corn that they might pick up in the fields.

The authorities at Washington watched Lee's movement with mingled feelings of anxiety and relief. They were relieved because he was evidently not aiming at the national capital. They were alarmed because the real point of attack was unknown. Sixty thousand men, flushed with triumph and under seemingly invincible leadership were headed somewhere, and as the rumor spread that that "somewhere" was Harrisburg or Philadelphia, the North stood aghast with consternation.

Face to face with this desperate crisis, McClellan, who had been practically removed from command, was restored to duty and given charge of all the Union forces in the field. Had he been invested with supreme authority, at least one grievous blunder might have been avoided, for as he proceeded to the front, calling loudly as usual for reenforcements, he advised the evacuation of Harper's Ferry, garrisoned by some 12,000 men who were exposed to capture by Lee's advance on Frederick City. But Halleck rejected this advice and on September 15, 1862, "Stonewall" Jackson, with about 20,000 men, swooped down upon the defenseless post and gobbled up almost the entire garrison with all its guns and stores. To accomplish this, however, he was forced to separate himself from Lee, and while McClellan, with over 87,000 men, was protesting that his opponent had 120,000 and that it was impossible to win against such odds, Lee's strength had been reduced to about 35,000 and his safety absolutely depended upon his adversary's fears. It was hardly to be hoped, however, that McClellan's imagination would cause him to see three men for every one opposed to him, but such was the fact, and even when one of Lee's confidential orders fell into his hands, revealing the fact that Jackson's whole force was absent, he still thought himself outnumbered.

The discovery of this order was a serious blow to Lee, for it not only exposed his immediate weakness, but actually disclosed his entire plan. How it was lost has never been explained, for its importance was so fully realized that one of the officers who received a copy pinned it in the inside pocket of his coat, another memorized his copy and then chewed it up and others took similar precautions to protect its secret.

Some officer, however, must have been careless, for when the Union troops halted at Frederick City, through which the Confederates had just passed, a private in an Indiana regiment found it lying on the ground wrapped around some cigars and, recognizing its value, carried it straight to his superiors who promptly bore it to Headquarters.

Had Lee remained ignorant of this discovery it is possible that McClellan might have effected the capture of his army. But a civilian, favoring the South who happened to be present when the paper reached Headquarters, slipped through the Union lines and put the Confederate commander on his guard.

Lee had already noted that McClellan was moving toward him at unusual speed for so cautious an officer and, this was readily explained by the news that his plans were known and Jackson's absence discovered. He accordingly posted his troops so that he could form a junction with the rest of the army at the earliest possible moment and halted in the vicinity of Sharpsburg near Antietam Creek.

Chapter XVIII
The Battle of Antietam or Sharpsburg

Had McClellan not absurdly overestimated the number of troops opposed to him when his army neared Sharpsburg on the 15th of September, 1862, he might have defeated Lee and possibly destroyed or captured his entire force. Never before had a Union commander had such an opportunity to deliver a crushing blow. He had more than 80,000 men under his control--fully twice as many as his adversary; he had the Confederate plan of campaign in his hands and such fighting as had occurred with the exception of that at Harper's Ferry had been decidedly in his favor. Moreover, Lee had recently met with a serious accident, his horse having knocked him down and trampled on him, breaking the bones of one hand, and otherwise injuring him so severely that he had been obliged to superintend most of the posting of his army from an ambulance. By a curious coincidence, too, "Stonewall" Jackson had been hurt in a similar manner a few days previously, so that if the battle had begun promptly, it is highly probable that he, too, would have been physically handicapped, and it is certain that his troops could not have reached the field in time to be of any assistance.

To Lee's immense relief, however, McClellan made no serious attack on either the 15th or 16th of September, but spent those two days in putting his finishing touches on his preparations, and before he completed them that Opportunity "which knocks but once at each man's gate" had passed him by, never to return.

The battle of Antietam or Sharpsburg began at dawn of the 17th, but by that time Jackson had arrived and both he and Lee had so far recovered from their injuries that they were able to be in the saddle and personally direct the movements of their men. The Confederate position had been skillfully selected for defense on the hills back of Antietam Creek and McClellan's plan was to break through his opponent's line, gain his rear and cut him off from retreat. But Lee, who had closely watched the elaborate massing of the Union forces for this attempt, was fully prepared for it and the first assault against his line was repulsed with fearful slaughter. No subtle strategy or brilliant tactics of any kind marked McClellan's conduct of the battle. Time and again he hurled his heavy battalions against his opponent's left, center and right in a desperate effort to pierce the wall of gray, and once or twice his heroic veterans almost succeeded in battering their way through. But at every crisis Lee rose to the emergency and moved his regiments as a skillful chess player manipulates his pieces on the board, now massing his troops at the danger point and now diverting his adversary's attack by a swift counter-stroke delivered by men unacquainted with defeat. Both his hands were heavily swathed in bandages and far too painful to admit of his even touching the bridle rein, but he had had himself lifted into the saddle and for fully fourteen hours he remained mounted on "Traveller," his famous war horse, watching every movement with the inspiring calmness of a commander born to rule the storm.

The situation was perilous and no one realized its dangers more keenly than he, but not a trace of anxiety appeared upon his face. Only twice was he betrayed into an expression of his feelings, once when he asked General Hood where the splendid division was which he had commanded in the morning and received the reply: "They are lying in the field where you sent them," and again when he directed the Rockbridge battery to go into action for a second time after three of its four guns had been disabled. The captain of this battery had halted to make a report of its condition and receive instructions, and Lee, gazing at the group of begrimed and tattered privates behind the officer, ordered them to renew their desperate work before he recognized that among them stood his youngest son, Robert.

Very few men in the Confederate commander's position would have suffered a son to serve in the ranks. A word from him would, of course, have made the boy an officer. But that was not Lee's way. To advance an inexperienced lad over the heads of older men was, to his mind, unjust and he would not do it even for his own flesh and blood. Nor had his son himself expected it, for he had eagerly accepted his father's permission to enter the ranks and had cheerfully performed his full duty, never presuming on his relationship to the Commander-in-Chief or asking favors of any kind. All this was known to Lee but this unexpected meeting at a moment when privates were being mowed down like grass was a terrible shock and strain. Nevertheless, it was characteristic of the man that no change was made in the orders of the Rockbridge battery, which continued on its way to the post of danger and, with young Lee, gallantly performed the work he had called on it to do.

By night the Confederates still held the field, but the struggle had cost them nearly 11,000 men, reducing their force to less than 45,000, while McClellan, despite even heavier losses, had more than 74,000 left. Lee, accordingly, withdrew his army under cover of darkness to another part of the field and again awaited attack. But McClellan neither attacked nor attempted anything like a pursuit until his opponent was safely out of reach, being well satisfied with having checked the advance of his formidable foe and spoiled his plans. This he was certainly entitled to claim, for Lee's campaign against Maryland and Pennsylvania was effectually balked by his enforced retreat.

Indeed, it is quite possible that had McClellan been adventurous he might have ended the war at Antietam, for the day after the battle he outnumbered his opponents at least two to one and possessed enormous advantage in the way of equipment and supplies. But the Union commander, though he possessed a genius for army organization and knew the art of inspiring confidence in his men, was no match for Lee in the field, and he probably realized this. At all events, he displayed no anxiety to renew hostilities and when urged, and at last positively ordered to advance, he argued, protested, offered excuses for delay and in fact did everything but obey.

Weeks thus slipped by and finally Lee himself became impatient to know what his adversary was doing. He, accordingly, again summoned Stuart and ordered him to repeat the experiment of riding around the opposing army. News of this second, almost derisive defiance of McClellan soon reached the North, for Stuart, swiftly circling his right flank, suddenly appeared with 1,800 men at Chambersburg, Pennsylvania, terrorizing the country and destroying vast quantities of stores. Stern and indignant orders from Washington warned the Union Commander that this time he must not permit the daring troopers to escape. But only a few scouts were captured, and once more Stuart sped safely back to his chief with full information as to the strength and position of the Federal lines.

Even this did not arouse McClellan, and two more weeks of inaction passed before he again set his vast army in motion. But by this time, the demand for his dismissal had become clamorous and, on November 5, 1862, President Lincoln reluctantly removed him from command.

Chapter XIX
Lee against Burnside and Hooker

Lincoln had good reason for hesitating to change commanders, for, unsatisfactory as McClellan had proved, the President was by no means sure that any of his other generals would do better. In fact, with all his defects, there was much to be said in McClellan's favor. As an organizer of troops or chief of staff he had displayed talents of the highest possible order, transforming the armed mob which had flocked to the defense of the Union at the opening of the war into a well-drilled and disciplined army. That he had not accomplished much with this great engine of war after it had been constructed, had not been wholly his fault, for he had never been entirely free from interference at the hands of incompetent superiors, and he had had the misfortune to be pitted against a past master of the art of war. Moreover, he had been called to the chief command at a moment of panic and peril and, if he had not succeeded in defeating Lee, he had, at Antietam, given the North the only semblance of victory which it could claim in all its campaigning in the South. But that one taste of triumph had whetted the public appetite for more. Despite McClellan's continuous talk about the overpowering numbers of his foes, the supporters of the Union knew that they outmatched the Confederacy in men, arms, ships, money, and resources of every kind. They accordingly insisted that the immense army which had lain idle in its camps for almost two months after the drawn battle at Antietam should be set to work.

In response to this popular demand, General Ambrose Burnside was appointed to take McClellan's place, and a more utterly unfitted man for prosecuting a successful campaign against Lee could scarcely have been selected. He himself fully realized this. Indeed, he had already twice refused the chief command on the ground that he did not feel competent to conduct a great campaign. But the public, which had become disgusted with boasters, admired his modesty, and his preparations for carrying the war again into Virginia were followed with high hopes for his success. The officers of the army, however, did not share the popular confidence in their new chief and some of those highest in authority gave him only a half-hearted support.

But nothing could have saved Burnside's extraordinary campaign. Had he been assigned to lead a forlorn hope, regardless of consequences, his plan, if it can be called a plan, might have been justified, but under the existing circumstances it was reckless to the point of madness. His first moves, however, were characterized by an excess of caution and so slowly did he advance that before he was fairly started for the South, Lee blocked the road, concentrating his whole army on the hills behind the City of Fredericksburg in a position practically defying attack.

To attempt a direct assault against this fortress-like post was suicidal, but apparently no thought of maneuvering crossed Burnside's mind. His one idea was to brush aside the foe. But before he could even reach him his army had to cross the Rappahannock, a formidable river, and march over an open plain, absolutely at the mercy of its intrenched opponents, who could, as one of their artillery officers expressed it, "comb the ground" with their cannon. Nevertheless, into this death trap the Union troops were plunged on the 13th of December, 1862, and they advanced to destruction with a dash and courage that won the admiration of friends and foes alike. The result was, of course, inevitable. No human beings could withstand the storm of shot and shell which burst upon them, and though some of the devoted columns actually reached the foot of the Confederate breastworks, they could do no more, and over 12,000 men fell victims to the disastrous attack.

For once, Lee was at an utter loss to comprehend his adversary's plan. He could not believe that this wanton butchery of men was all there was to the contest. To his mind such an awful sacrifice of human life would never have been made unless for the purpose of paving the way for another enterprise absolutely certain of success. But nothing more was attempted and the battle of Fredericksburg, reflecting the conception of a disordered brain rather than the trained intelligence of a graduate of West Point, was added to the already long list of blunders which prolonged the war.

Burnside brought severe charges against several of his generals for their failure to support his sorry tactics, and even went so far as to demand their dismissal from the army. There was undoubtedly some ground for his complaints, but such obviously incompetent leadership was enough to demoralize any army, and not long after his crippled battalions retreated behind the Rappahannock he was relieved of his command, which was given to General Joseph Hooker, one of the officers he most seriously accused.

Hooker was familiarly known to the country as "Fighting Joe," a name he had well earned on many a hard-fought field. He, like his predecessors, was a graduate of West Point and his record, in many respects worthy of the best traditions of that famous school, inspired the army with the belief that it had, at last, found a leader who would pilot it to victory.

Certainly, the new commander was not troubled with Burnside's self-distrust. His confidence in himself and in his plans was unbounded, and there was no little justification for his hopes, for his campaign was well thought out and he had a force of over 130,000 men under his orders--fully 70,000 more than his adversary could bring into the field.

Lee still lay intrenched on the hills behind Fredericksburg, and there Hooker ordered General Sedgwick to hold him with part of the army while he himself, with another and more powerful part, crossed the Rappahannock River by a ford twenty-seven miles above. By this move he hoped to get behind Lee and then crush him, as nut-crackers would crush a nut, by closing in on him with a front and rear attack.

This was not a strikingly original plan. It was in fact merely a flanking movement on a huge scale, but compared to Burnside's performance it was highly scientific and the vast superiority of the Union forces almost insured its success. Hooker was certainly convinced that he had at last solved the great problem of the war and that Lee was practically in his power. Indeed, as his flanking army forded the river, he issued an address of congratulation in which he informed his troops that they had the Confederates in a position from which they must either "ingloriously fly" or come out in the open where certain defeat awaited them. But "Fighting Joe" was soon to learn the folly of crowing until one is out of the woods, for as he emerged from the forests sheltering the fords, he discovered that Lee's army had not remained tamely in its intrenchments, but had quietly slipped away and planted itself squarely across his path.

For a moment the Union commander was fairly astounded. He had prophesied that his adversary would fly from Fredericksburg, but he had not expected him to move so soon or in this direction. Indeed, his well-matured plans were based on the supposition that Lee would remain where he wanted him to be until he was ready to spring his trap, quite forgetting that though it is easy to catch birds after you have put salt on their tails, it is rather difficult to make them wait while you salt them. As a matter of fact, Lee had taken alarm the moment his cavalry scouts reported his opponent's movement towards the fords and, realizing that he would be caught if he remained where he was, he had rapidly departed from Fredericksburg, leaving only enough force to occupy Sedgwick's attention. Even then he was in a precarious position, for Hooker's flanking army alone outnumbered him and the force threatening Fredericksburg would certainly start in pursuit of him as soon as it discovered that the bulk of his army had withdrawn from that city. All this was equally clear to Hooker after his first gasp of astonishment, and as he hurriedly ordered Sedgwick to attack Fredericksburg with part of his forces and to send the rest as reenforcement against Lee, he confidently believed that his foe had delivered himself into his hands.

But Lee, though cornered, was not yet caught. He had to think and act quickly but though he had only 45,000 men and Hooker had 70,000 on the spot, his idea was not to escape but to attack. A close examination of the opposing lines in front and at the Federal left disclosed no weakness, but the right beyond Chancellorsville looked more hopeful. Then a brilliant idea suddenly occurred to his mind. The Union commander was evidently awaiting or meditating a direct attack and had no fear except that his prey might escape him. Might it not be possible to keep him busily occupied in front, while a force stole behind his right wing and caught it between two fires?

This was precisely what Hooker had been endeavoring to do to him, but Lee was well aware that what was safe for a large army might be ruinous for a small one and that his proposed maneuver would require him to divide his small army into two smaller parts, both of which would be annihilated if the move was discovered. But capture or destruction stared him in the face any way, so, learning from a certain Colonel Welford that a road used by him in former years for transporting materials to a local furnace could be utilized to swing a considerable force behind Hooker's right, he determined to take the desperate chance.

The necessary orders were accordingly issued during the night of May 1, 1863, and by daylight the next morning Jackson started off on the back trail with about 30,000 men, leaving Lee with only 15,000 to face Hooker's overwhelming array. The success of the whole enterprise depended upon the secrecy and speed with which it was conducted, but Jackson had already proved his ability in such work and his men set off at a brisk pace well screened by vigilant cavalry. It was not possible, however, wholly to conceal the march, and not long after it began several quite definite reports of its progress reached Hooker. But though he duly warned his Corps Commanders to be on their guard against a flank movement, he himself evidently interpreted it as the beginning of a retreat. Indeed, by four o'clock in the afternoon of May 2nd he became convinced that his victims were striving to escape, for he advised Sedgwick, "We know that the enemy is fleeing, trying to save his trains." But even as he dispatched this message Jackson was behind at the Union right and his men were forming in line of battle under cover of a heavy curtain of woods.

Meanwhile, some of the division commanders at the threatened position had become disquieted by the reports that a large body of Confederates was marching somewhere, though just where no one seemed to know. Two of them accordingly faced their men toward the rear in readiness for an attack from that direction. But the assurances which reached them from headquarters that the enemy was in full flight discouraged precautions of this kind, and when Jackson crept up a neighboring hill to examine the Union position, he found most of the troops had their backs turned to the point of danger. In fact, the camp, as a whole presented a most inviting spectacle, for the soldiers were scattered about it, playing cards or preparing their evening meal, with their arms stacked in the rear, little dreaming that one of their most dreaded foes was watching them from a hilltop, behind which crouched thousands of his men. Every detail of the scene was impressed on Jackson's memory when he quietly slipped back into the woods, and for the next two hours he busied himself posting his troops to the best advantage.

It was six o'clock when the order to attack was given and most of the Union soldiers were still at their suppers when deer, foxes, rabbits and other animals, alarmed by a mass of men advancing through the forest, began to tear through the camp as though fleeing from a prairie fire. But before the startled soldiers could ask an explanation of this strange stampede, the answer came in the form of a scattering musketry fire and the fearsome yells of 26,000 charging men.

The panic that followed beggars description. Regiments huddled against regiments in helpless confusion; artillery, infantry and cavalry became wedged in narrow roads and remained hopelessly jammed; officers and men fought with one another; generals were swept aside or carried forward on the human waves, hoarsely bellowing orders which no one heeded, while into the welter the Confederates poured a deadly fire and rounded up masses of bewildered prisoners. It was well-nigh dusk before even the semblance of a line of defense could be formed to cover the disorganized masses of men, but the gathering darkness increased the terror of the hapless fugitives, who, stumbling and crashing their way to safety, carried confusion in their wake.

Meanwhile Lee, advised of what was happening at the Union right, vigorously attacked Hooker's left, and a fierce conflict at that point added to the general turmoil until the contending forces could no longer distinguish each other, save by the flashing of their guns. The fighting then ceased all along the line and both sides busied themselves with preparations for renewing the struggle at the earliest possible moment. Jackson, accompanied by some of his staff, instantly began a reconnoissance of the Union position. He had just completed this and was returning to his lines when some of his own pickets, mistaking his party for Union cavalry, fired on them killing a captain and a sergeant. The Confederate commander immediately turned his horse and sought safety at another point, but he had not progressed far before he drew the fire of another picket squad and fell desperately wounded.

General A. P. Hill then assumed command, but fighting had scarcely been resumed the next morning before he was wounded and Jeb Stuart took his place. Meanwhile, Hooker had been injured and the next day Lee fiercely assailed Sedgwick. For the best part of two days the battle raged with varying success. But, little by little, the Confederates edged their opponents toward the Rappahannock, and by the night of May 5th, 1863, Hooker withdrew his exhausted forces across the river.

The battle of Chancellorsville cost Lee over 12,000 men; but with a force which never exceeded 60,000, he had not only extricated himself from a perilous position, but had inflicted a crushing blow on an army of 130,000, an achievement which has passed into history as one of the most brilliant feats of modern warfare.

Chapter XX
In the Hour of Triumph

Great as Lee's reputation had been before the battle of Chancellorsville, it was immensely increased by that unexpected triumph. But no trace of vanity or self-gratulation of any kind marked his reception of the chorus of praise that greeted him. On the contrary, he modestly disclaimed the honors from the very first and insisted that to Jackson belonged the credit of the day. "Could I have directed events," he wrote the wounded General, "I should have chosen to have been disabled in your stead. I congratulate you on the victory which is due to your skill and energy." Indeed, when the news first reached him that Jackson's left arm had been amputated, he sent him a cheery message, saying, "You are better off than I am, for while you have only lost your LEFT, I have lost my RIGHT arm." And when, at last, he learned that "Stonewall" had passed away, he no longer thought of the victory but only of his dead comrade and friend. "Any victory would be dear at such a price," was his sorrowful comment on the day.

Jackson was indeed Lee's "right arm" and his place among the great captains of the world is well indicated by the fact that a study of his campaign is to-day part of the education of all English and American officers. Nevertheless, it was unquestionably Lee's genius that enabled his great Lieutenant to accomplish what he did, and this Jackson himself fully realized. "Better that ten Jacksons should fall than one Lee," was his response to his commander's generous words.

But though Lee had won an international reputation, anyone seeing him in the field among his soldiers might well have imagined that he was wholly unaware that the world was ringing with his fame. He steadily declined all offers to provide comfortable quarters for his accommodation, preferring to live in a simple tent and share with his men the discomforts of the field. Indeed, his thoughts were constantly of others, never of himself, and when gifts of fruit and other dainties for his table were tendered him, he thanked the givers but suggested that they were needed for the sick and wounded in the hospitals, where they would be gratefully received.

"...I should certainly have endeavored to throw the enemy north of the Potomac," he wrote his wife, "but thousands of our men were barefooted, thousands with fragments of shoes, and all without overcoats, blankets or warm clothing. I could not bear to expose them to certain suffering.... I am glad you have some socks for the army. Send them to me.... Tell the girls to send all they can. I wish they could make some shoes, too."

Even the hardships of the dumb animals moved him to a ready sympathy, and he was constantly planning to spare them in every possible way.

"Our horses and mules suffer most," he wrote one of his daughters. "They have to bear the cold and rain, tug through the mud and suffer all the time with hunger."

And again on another occasion he wrote his wife:

"This morning the whole country is covered with a mantle of snow, fully a foot deep.... Our poor horses were enveloped. We have dug them out...but it will be terrible.... I fear our short rations for man and horse will have to be curtailed."

The whole army realized the great-hearted nature of its Chief, and its confidence in his thought and care is well illustrated by a letter which a private addressed to him, asking him if he knew upon what short rations the men were living. If he did, the writer stated, their privations were doubtless necessary and everyone would cheerfully accept them, knowing that he had the comfort of his men continually in mind.

War had no illusions for this simple, God-fearing man. He regarded it as a terrible punishment for the shortcomings of mankind. For him it had no glory.

"The country here looks very green and pretty, notwithstanding the ravages of war," he wrote his wife. "What a beautiful world God, in His loving kindness to His creatures, has given us! What a shame that men endowed with reason and knowledge of right should mar His gifts."

The awful responsibility of his public duty was almost more than any man could bear, but he had also to endure personal anxiety and sorrow of the keenest kind. During his absence in the field one of his daughters died, his wife was in failing health and his three sons were in the army daily exposed to injury and death. Fitzhugh and Custis had been made generals, and Robert had been promoted to a lieutenancy and assigned to his elder brother's staff. Up to the battle of Chancellorsville they had escaped unharmed, but while the contending armies lay watching each other on either side of the Rappahannock, Fitzhugh was severely wounded in a cavalry engagement and Lee's first thought was to comfort and reassure the young man's wife.

"I am so grieved," ...he wrote her, "to send Fitzhugh to you wounded.... With his youth and strength to aid him, and your tender care to nurse him, I trust he will soon be well again. I know that you will unite with me in thanks to Almighty God, who has so often sheltered him in the hour of danger."

Then came the news that the young General had been captured by Federal troops who surrounded the house to which he had been removed, and again Lee sought, in the midst of all his cares, to cheer his daughter-in-law who was herself becoming ill.

"I can see no harm that can result from Fitzhugh's capture except his detention.... He will be in the hands of old army officers and surgeons, most of whom are men of principle and humanity. His wound, I understand, has not been injured by his removal, but is doing well. Nothing would do him more harm than for him to learn that you were sick and sad. How could he get well? So cheer up and prove your fortitude.... You may think of Fitzhugh and love him as much as you please, but do not grieve over him or grow sad."

But the young wife grew steadily worse and, when her life was despaired of, Custis Lee offered to take his brother's place in prison, if the authorities would allow him to visit his dying wife. But, when this was refused and news of her death reached Lee, he refrained from all bitterness.

"...I grieve," he wrote his wife, "...as a father only can grieve for a daughter, and my sorrow is heightened by the thought of the anguish her death will cause our dear son, and the poignancy it will give to the bars of his prison. May God in His mercy enable him to bear the blow...."

It was in the midst of such severe afflictions that Lee conducted some of the most important moves of his campaign, and while family anxieties were beginning to crowd on him, the condition of his army and the political situation were already demanding another invasion of the North. As far as spirit and discipline were concerned, his troops were never more ready for active service and their numbers had been so considerably increased during the weeks that followed the battle of Chancellorsville that by the 1st of June, 1863, he could count on almost 70,000 fairly well-armed men, supported by over two hundred cannon.

But the question of supplying food for this great array was every day becoming more urgent, and the remark of the Commissary-General that his Chief would soon have to seek his provisions in Pennsylvania was significant of the situation. Lee thoroughly realized that the strength of the Confederacy was waning and that unless some great success in the field should soon force the Union to make terms, the end of the struggle was in sight. Great victories had already been won, but always on Southern soil, and the news that Grant was closing in on Vicksburg demanded that a supreme effort be made to offset that impending disaster in the West.

If the Southern army could force its way into the North and there repeat its triumphs, England and France would probably recognize the Confederacy and the half-hearted supporters of the Union, already murmuring against the war, would clamor for peace. With this idea Lee devoted the month following the battle of Chancellorsville to recruiting his strength and watching for some move on Hooker's part. But Hooker remained quietly within his lines, so on June 3, 1863, his opponent, concealing his purpose, moved rapidly and secretly toward Pennsylvania.

Chapter XXI
Grant at Vicksburg

While Lee had been disposing of McClellan, Pope and Burnside, Grant had remained in comparative idleness near Corinth, Mississippi. He had, it is true, been assigned to high command in the West when Halleck was ordered to Washington, but the battle of Shiloh had prejudiced the authorities against him and his troops were gradually transferred to other commanders, leaving him with an army barely sufficient to guard the territory it already held. This treatment seriously depressed him and with plenty of time to brood over his troubles, he was in some danger of lapsing into the bad habits which had once had such a fatal hold upon him. But at this crisis his wife was by his side to steady and encourage him, and the Confederates soon diverted his thoughts from his own grievances by giving him plenty of work to keep them at arm's length. Meanwhile, however, something much more disturbing occurred, for he suddenly discovered that preparations were being made to place his long-cherished campaign for the opening of the Mississippi River in the hands of McClernand, the political General whose conduct at Fort Donelson had demonstrated his ignorance of military affairs.

That aroused Grant to action and hastily summoning Admiral Porter and General Sherman to his aid, he started towards Vicksburg, Mississippi, on November 2, 1862, determined to be the first in the field and thus head off any attempt to displace him from the command.

McClernand's project was accordingly nipped in the bud, for, of course, he could not be authorized to conduct a campaign already undertaken by a superior officer, and the troops which had been intended for him were immediately forwarded to Grant. Doubtless, the President was not displeased at this turn of affairs, for although McClernand was a highly important person in the political world and had rendered valuable services in raising troops, his defects as a general were widely recognized, and there had been grave doubts as to the wisdom of permitting him to attempt so difficult an undertaking as the capture of Vicksburg. Within a few months, however, there were even graver doubts as to the wisdom of having entrusted the enterprise to Grant, for by the end of March, 1863, the general opinion was that no one could have made a worse mess of it than he was making, and that it was hopeless to expect anything as long as he was in authority.

As a matter of fact, the immense difficulty of capturing a city such as Vicksburg had not been realized until the work was actually undertaken. It was practically a fortress commanding the Mississippi, and whoever held it ruled the river. The Confederate leaders understood this very thoroughly and they had accordingly fortified the place, which was admirably adapted for defense, with great care and skill. In front of it flowed the Mississippi, twisting and turning in such snake-like conditions that it could be navigated only by boats of a certain length and build, and on either side of the city stretched wide swamp lands and bayous completely commanded by batteries well posted on the high ground occupied by the town. All this was formidable enough in itself, but shortly after Grant began his campaign, the river overflowed its banks and the whole country for miles was under water which, while not deep enough for steamers, was an absolute barrier to the approach of an army.

Indeed, the capture of the city seemed hopeless from a military standpoint, but Grant would not abandon the task. Finding traces of an abandoned canal, he attempted to complete it in the hope of changing the course of the river, or at least of diverting some of the water from the overflowed land, but the effort was a stupendous failure almost from the start. Then he ordered the levees of the Mississippi protecting two great lakes to be cut, with the idea of flooding the adjacent streams and providing a waterway for his ships. This gigantic enterprise was actually put into operation, the dams were removed, and gun-boats were forced on the swollen watercourses far into the interior until some of them became hopelessly tangled in the submerged forests and their crews, attacked by the Confederate sharpshooters, were glad to make their escape. Week after week and month after month this exhausting work continued, but, at the end of it all, Vicksburg was no nearer capture than before. Indeed, the only result of the campaign was the loss of thousands of men who died of malaria, yellow fever, smallpox, and all the diseases which swamp lands breed. For this, of course, Grant was severely criticized and the denunciations at last became so bitter that an order removing him from the command was entrusted to an official who was directed to deliver it, if, on investigation, the facts seemed to warrant it.

But the visiting official, after arriving at the front, soon learned that the army had complete confidence in its commander and that it would be a mistake to interfere with him. Indeed, by this time "the silent General," who had neither answered the numerous complaints against him nor paid the least attention to the storm of public indignation raging beyond his camp, had abandoned his efforts to reach Vicksburg from the front and was busily engaged in swinging his army behind it by a long overland route in the face of appalling difficulties, but with a grim resolution which forced all obstructions from his path. Meanwhile, the gun-boats under Admiral Porter were ordered to attempt to run the land batteries, and April 16, 1863, was selected as the date for their perilous mission. Each vessel had been carefully protected by cotton bales, and the crews stood ready with great wads of cotton to stop leaks, while all lights were extinguished except one in the stern of each ship to guide the one that followed.

It was a black night when the Admiral started down the river in his flagship, and for a while it was hoped that the fleet would slip by the batteries under cover of darkness. The leading vessels did, indeed, escape the lookouts of the first forts, but before long a warning rocket shot into the sky and the river was instantly lit by immense bonfires which had been prepared for just this emergency, and by the glare of their flames the gunners poured shot and shell at the black hulls as they sped swiftly by. Shot after shot found its mark, but still the fleet continued on its course. Then, after the bonfires died down, houses were set on fire to enable the artillerists to see their targets, but before daylight the whole fleet had run the gauntlet and lay almost uninjured below Vicksburg, ready to cooperate with Grant's advancing army.

By this time the Confederates must have realized that they were facing defeat. Nevertheless, for fully a month they stubbornly contested every foot of ground. But Grant, approaching the rear by his long, roundabout marches, handled his veteran troops with rare good judgment, moving swiftly and allowing his adversaries no rest, so that by the 17th of May, 1863, General Pemberton, commanding the defenses of Vicksburg, was forced to take refuge in the town. Grant immediately swung his army into position, blocking every avenue of escape and began a close siege. The prize for which he had been struggling for more than half a year was now fairly within his grasp, but there was still a chance that it might slip through his fingers, for close on his heels came General Joseph Johnston with a powerful army intent upon rescuing General Pemberton and his gallant garrison.

If Johnston could come to Pemberton's relief or if Pemberton could break through and unite with Johnston, they could together save Vicksburg. But Grant had resolved that they should not join forces, and to the problem confronting him he devoted himself body and mind. Constantly in the saddle, watching every detail of the work as the attacking army slowly dug its way toward the city and personally posting the troops holding Johnston at bay, his quiet, determined face and mud-splashed uniform became familiar sights to the soldiers, and his appearance on the lines was invariably greeted with inspiring cheers. By July, the trenches of the besieged and the besiegers were so close together that the opposing pickets could take to each other, and the gun-boats threw shells night and day into the town. Still Pemberton would not surrender and many of the inhabitants of Vicksburg were forced to leave their houses and dig caves in the cliffs upon which the city was built to protect themselves and their families from the iron hail.

It was only when food of every kind had been practically exhausted and his garrison was threatened with starvation that Pemberton yielded. On July 3, 1863, however, he realized that the end had come and raised the white flag. Nearly twenty-four hours passed before the terms of surrender were agreed upon, but Grant, who had served in the same division with Pemberton in the Mexican War, was not inclined to exact humiliating conditions upon his old acquaintance whose men had made such a long and gallant fight. He, accordingly, offered to free all the prisoners upon their signing a written promise not to take arms again unless properly exchanged, and to allow all the officers to retain their side arms and horses. These generous terms were finally accepted, and on July 4, 1863, the Confederate army, numbering about 30,000, marched out in the presence of their opponents and stacked their arms, receiving the tribute of absolute silence from the 75,000 men who watched them from the Union ranks.

Four months before this event, Halleck, the Commander-in-Chief, had advised Grant and other officers of his rank that there was a major generalship in the Regular Army for the man who should first win a decisive victory in the field. The captor of Vicksburg had certainly earned this promotion, for with its fall the Mississippi River was controlled by the Union and, in the words of Lincoln, "The Father of Waters again ran unvexed to the sea."

Chapter XXII
The Battle of Gettysburg

The news that Grant was slowly, but surely, tightening his grip upon Vicksburg, and that nothing but an accident could prevent its capture, was known to the whole country for fully a week before the surrender occurred, but it neither encouraged the North nor discouraged the South. To the minds of many people no victory in the West could save the Union, for Lee was already in Pennsylvania, sweeping northward toward Harrisburg and Philadelphia, and even threatening New York. Hooker, in the field, and Halleck, in Washington, were squabbling as to what should be done, and the Union army was groping blindly after the invaders without any leadership worthy of the name.

It was certainly a critical moment demanding absolute harmony on the part of the Union leaders; but while the fate of the Union trembled in the balance, Hooker and Halleck wrangled and contradicted each other, apparently regardless of consequences, and the climax of this disgraceful exhibition was a petulant telegram from Hooker (June 27, 1863) resigning his command. Had "Fighting Joe" been the greatest general in the world this resignation, in the presence of the enemy, would have ruined his reputation, and the moment President Lincoln accepted it Hooker was a discredited man.

To change commanders at such a crisis was a desperately perilous move, but the President knew that the army had lost confidence in its leader since the battle of Chancellorsville and the fact that he could even think of resigning on the eve of a battle demonstrated his utter unfitness for the task at hand. It was, therefore, with something of relief that Lincoln ordered General Meade to take immediate charge of all the troops in the field, and the new commander assumed the responsibility in these words, "As a soldier I obey the order placing me in command of this army and to the utmost of my ability will execute it."

At the moment he dispatched this manly and modest response to the unexpected call to duty, Meade knew little of Hooker's plans and had only a vague idea of where his troops were posted. Under such conditions success in the coming battle was almost impossible, but he wasted no time in complaints or excuses, but instantly began to move his forces northward to incept the line of Lee's advance. Even up to this time, however, the exact position of the Confederate army had not been ascertained, for Lee had concealed his infantry behind his cavalry, which effectually prevented his adversaries from getting near enough to discover the direction of his march.

Another "cavalry screen," however, covered the Union forces and though Lee dispatched Stuart to break through and discover what lay behind it, the daring officer for once failed to accomplish his purpose and Lee had to proceed without the information he usually possessed. This was highly advantageous to Meade, for his forces were badly scattered and had Lee known that fact he might have crushed the various parts of the army before they united, or at least have prevented some of them from reaching the field in time. He soon learned, of course, that Meade had taken Hooker's place, but if he had not heard the news directly, he would have guessed that some great change had occurred in the generalship of his opponents, for within twenty-four hours of his appointment Meade had his army well in hand, and two days later the rapid and skillful concentration of his force was clear to Lee's experienced eyes. By this time both armies had passed beyond their cavalry screens, and on the 30th of June, 1863, the advance of the Confederate troops neared the little town of Gettysburg.

But Lee was not yet ready to fight, for, although he was better prepared than his adversary, he wanted to select the best possible ground before joining battle. By a strange chance, however, it was not Lee but his bare-footed followers who decided where the battle should be fought, for as his advance-guard approached Gettysburg one of the brigade commanders asked and received permission from his superior to enter the town and procure shoes for his men. But Gettysburg was found to be occupied by Union cavalry and the next day (July 1st) a larger force was ordered forward to drive them away and "get the shoes." Meanwhile, the Union cavalry had been reenforced and, to offset this, more Confederates were ordered to the support of their comrades. Once more Union reenforcements were hurried to the front, and again the Confederates responded to the challenge, until over 50,000 men were engaged in a savage conflict, and before noon the battle of Gettysburg, one of the greatest battles of history, had begun.

The men in gray, who thus unwittingly forced the fighting, were veterans of many campaigns and they attacked with a fury that carried all before them. The Union troops fought with courage, but General Reynolds, their commander, one of the ablest officers in the army, was soon shot through the head and instantly killed, and from that moment the Confederates crowded them to the point of panic. Indeed, two of Meade's most effective fighting corps were practically annihilated and the shattered remnants of the defenders of Gettysburg were hurled through the town in headlong flight toward what was known as Cemetery Hill, where their new commander, General Hancock, found them huddled in confusion.

Meade had displayed good judgment in selecting Hancock to take Reynolds' place, for he was just the man to inspire confidence in the disheartened soldiers and rise to the emergency that confronted him. But, though he performed wonders in the way of restoring order and encouraging his men to make a desperate resistance, it is more than probable that the Confederates would have swept the field and gained the important position of Cemetery Hill had they followed up their victory. Fortunately for the Union cause, however, the pursuit was not continued much beyond the limits of Gettysburg and, as though well satisfied to have got the shoes they came for, the victors contented themselves with the undisputed possession of the town.

Neither Lee nor Meade took any part in this unexpected battle, but Lee arrived during the afternoon while the Union troops were in full flight for the hills and, seeing the opportunity of delivering a crushing blow, advised Ewell, the commanding General, to pursue. His suggestion, however, was disregarded, and being unwilling to interfere with another officer in the midst of an engagement, he did not give a positive order, with the result that Cemetery Hill was left in possession of the Federal troops. Meanwhile Meade, having learned of the situation, was hurrying to the scene of action, where he arrived late at night, half dead with exhaustion and on the verge of nervous collapse from the fearful responsibilities which had been heaped upon him during the previous days. But the spirit of the man rose superior to his physical weakness and, keeping his head in the whirlwind of hurry and confusion, he issued orders rushing every available man to the front, made a careful examination of the ground and chose an admirable position for defense.

To this inspiring example the whole army made a magnificent response, and before the 2nd of July dawned the widely scattered troops began pouring in and silently moving into position for the desperate work confronting them. Meade had determined to await an attack from Lee and he had accordingly selected Cemetery Ridge as the position best adapted for defense. This line of hills not only provided a natural breastwork, but at the left and a little in front lay two hillocks knows as Round Top and Little Round Top, which, when crowned by artillery, were perfect fortresses of strength. Strange as it may seem, however, Round Top was not immediately occupied by the Union troops and had it not been for the quick eye and prompt action of General Warren, Little Round Top, the key to the entire Union position, would have been similarly neglected.

Lee was reasonably assured, at the end of the first day's fighting, that his adversary had not succeeded in getting all his troops upon the field and, realizing what an advantage this gave him, he determined to begin the battle at daylight, before the Union reenforcements could arrive. But for once, at least, the great commander received more objections than obedience from his subordinates, General Longstreet, one of his most trusted lieutenants, being the principal offender. Longstreet had, up to this moment, made a splendid record in the campaigns and Lee had such confidence in his skill that he seldom gave him a peremptory order, finding that a suggestion carried all the weight of a command. But, on this occasion, Longstreet did not agree with the Chief's plan of battle and he accordingly took advantage of the discretion reposed in him to postpone making an attack until he received a sharp and positive order to put his force in action. By this time, the whole morning had passed and every hour had brought more and more Union troops into the field, so that by the afternoon Meade had over 90,000 men opposing Lee's 70,000 veterans.

There was nothing half-hearted about Longstreet once he was in motion and the struggle for the possession of Little Round Top was as desperate a conflict as was ever waged on any field. Again and again the gray regiments hurled themselves into the very jaws of death to gain the coveted vantage ground, and again and again the blue lines, torn, battered and well-nigh crushed to earth, re-formed and hurled back the assault. Dash and daring were met by courage and firmness, and at nightfall, though the Confederates had gained some ground, their opponents still held their original position. Both sides had paid dearly, however, for whatever successes they had gained, the Union army alone having lost at least 20,000 men [Note from Brett: While this is possible, it is highly unlikely as the total casualties for the three day battle from the Unionist side were 23,053 according to official records. Current (circa 2000) estimates are that both sides lost about 9,000 soldiers on this day.]. Indeed, the Confederate attack had been so formidable that Meade called a council of war at night to determine whether the army should remain where it was for another day or retreat to a still stronger position. The council, however, voted unanimously to "stay and fight it out," and the next morning (July 3rd) saw the two armies facing each other in much the same positions as they had occupied the day before, the Unionists crowding the heights of Cemetery Ridge and the Confederates holding the hills known as Seminary Ridge and clinging to the bases of Round Top and Little Round Top, to which point the tide of valor had carried them.

A mile of valley and undulating slopes separated Cemetery Hill from Seminary Ridge, and their crests were crowded with artillery when the sun rose on July 3, 1863. But for a time the battle was confined to the infantry, the Confederates continuing fierce assaults of the previous evening. Then, suddenly, all their troops were withdrawn, firing ceased and absolute silence ensued along their whole lines. At an utter loss to understand this complete disappearance of the foe, the Union commanders peered through their glasses at the silent and apparently deserted heights of Seminary Ridge, growing more and more nervous as time wore on. What was the explanation of this ominous silence? Was it possible that Lee had retreated? Was he trying to lure them out of their position and catch them in some giant ambuscade? Was he engaged in a flanking movement such as had crumpled them to pieces at Chancellorsville? Doubtless, more than one soldier shot an apprehensive glance toward the rear during the strange hush as he remembered the terrifying appearance of Jackson on that fearful day.

But no Jackson stood at Lee's right hand, and suddenly two sharp reports rang out from the opposing height. Then, in answer to this signal, came the crash of a hundred and thirty cannon and instantly eighty Union guns responded to the challenge with a roar which shook the earth, while the air was filled with exploding shells and the ground was literally ploughed with shot. For an hour and a half this terrific duel continued; and then the Union chief of artillery, seeing that his supply of ammunition was sinking, ordered the guns to cease firing and the Confederates, believing that they had completely demolished the opposing batteries, soon followed their example. Another awful silence ensued and when the Union troops peered cautiously from behind the stone walls and slopes which had completely protected them from the wild storm of shot and shell, they saw a sight which filled them with admiration and awe.

From the woods fringing the opposing heights 15,000 men [Note from Brett: (circa 2000) just under 12,000 men] were sweeping in perfect order with battle flags flying, bayonets glistening and guidons fluttering as though on dress parade. Well to the front rode a gallant officer with a cap perched jauntily over his right ear and his long auburn hair hanging almost to his shoulders flying in the wind. This was General Pickett, and he and the men behind him had almost a mile of open ground to cross in the charge which was to bring them immortal fame. For half the distance they moved triumphantly forward, unscathed by the already thundering artillery, and then the Union cannon which had apparently been silenced by the Confederate fire began to pour death and destruction into their ranks. Whole rows of men were mowed down by the awful cannonade, but their comrades pressed forward undismayed, halting for a moment under cover of a ravine to re-form their ranks and then springing on again with a heroism unsurpassed in the history of war. A hail of bullets from the Union trenches fairly staggered them, yet on and on they charged. Once they actually halted in the face of the blazing breastworks, deliberately fired a volley and came on again with a rush, seized some of the still smoking guns that had sought to annihilate them and, beating back the gunners in a hand-to-hand conflict, actually planted their battle flags on the crest of Cemetery Ridge. Then the whole Union army seemed to leap from the ground and hurl itself upon them. They reeled, turned, broke into fragments and fled, leaving 5,000 dead and wounded in their trail.

Such was Pickett's charge--a wave of human courage which recorded "the high-water mark of the Rebellion."

Chapter XXIII
In the Face of Disaster

As the survivors of Pickett's heroic legion came streaming back toward the Confederate lines Lee stood face to face with defeat for the first time in his career. His long series of victories had not spoiled him and the hour of triumph had always found him calm and thankful, rather than elated and arrogant. But many a modest and generous winner has proved himself a poor loser. It is the moment of adversity that tries men's souls and revels the greatness or smallness of character, and subjected to this test more than one commander in the war had been found wanting. McClellan, staggering from his campaign against Richmond, blamed almost everyone but himself for the result; Pope, scurrying toward the fortifications of Washington, was as ready with excuses as he had been with boasts; Burnside, reeling from the slaughter-pen of Fredericksburg, had demanded the dismissal of his principal officers, and Hooker hurled accusations right and left in explaining the Chancellorsville surprise.

But Lee resorted neither to accusation nor excuse for the battle of Gettysburg. With the tide of disaster sweeping relentlessly down upon him, he hastened to assume entire responsibility for the result. "It is all my fault," he exclaimed, as the exhausted and shattered troops were seeking shelter from the iron hail, and then as calmly and firmly as though no peril threatened, he strove to rally the disorganized fugitives and present a bold front to the foe. It was no easy task, even with a veteran army, to prevent a panic and restore order and confidence in the midst of the uproar and confusion of defeat, but the quiet dignity and perfect control of their commander steadied the men, and at sight of him even the wounded raised themselves from the ground and cheered.

"All this will come right in the end," he assured the wavering troops, as he passed among them. "We'll talk it over afterwards, but in the meantime all good men must rally."

Not a sign of excitement or alarm was to be detected in his face, as he issued his orders and moved along the lines. "All this has been my fault," he repeated soothingly to a discouraged officer. "It is I that have lost this fight and you must help me out of it the best way you can.... Don't whip your horse, Captain," he quietly remarked, as he noted another officer belaboring his mount for shying at an exploding shell.... "I've got just another foolish horse myself, and whipping does no good."

Nothing escaped his watchful eyes, nothing irritated him, and nothing provoked him to hasty words or actions. Completely master of himself, he rose superior to the whirling storm about him and, commanding order out of chaos, held his shattered army under such perfect control that had Meade rushed forward in pursuit he might have met with a decisive check.

But Meade did not attempt to leave his intrenchments and the Confederate army slowly and defiantly moved toward the South. The situation was perilous--desperately perilous for Lee. His troops were in no condition to fight after battling for three days, their ammunition was almost exhausted, their food supply was low and they were retreating through a hostile country with a victorious army behind them and a broad river in their path. But not a man in the gray ranks detected even a shadow of anxiety on his commander's face, and when the Potomac was reached and it was discovered that the river was impassable owing to an unexpected flood, the army faced about and awaited attack with sublime confidence in the powers of its chief.

Meanwhile Meade, who had been cautiously following his adversary, began to receive telegrams and dispatches urging him to throw himself upon the Confederates before they could recross the Potomac and thus end the war. But this, in the opinion of the Union commander, was easier said than done, and he continued to advance with the utmost deliberation while Lee, momentarily expecting attack, ferried his sick and wounded across the river and prepared for a desperate resistance. Absolute ruin now stared him in the face, for no reenforcements of any kind could reach him and a severe engagement would soon place him completely at his opponent's mercy. Nevertheless, he presented a front so menacing and unafraid that when Meade called his officers to a council of war all but two voted against risking an attack.

In the meantime the river began to fall, and without the loss of a moment Lee commenced building a bridge across which his troops started to safety on the night of July 13th, ten days after the battle. Even then the situation was perilous in the extreme, for had Meade discovered the movement in time he could undoubtedly have destroyed a large part of the retreating forces, but when he appeared on the scene practically the whole army was on the other side of the river and only a few stragglers fell into his hands.

Great as Lee's success had been he never appeared to better advantage than during this masterly retreat, when, surrounded by difficulties and confronted by overwhelming numbers, he held his army together and led it to safety. Through the dust of defeat he loomed up greater as a man and greater as a soldier than at any other moment of his career.

Even the decisive victories at Gettysburg and Vicksburg failed to offset President Lincoln's bitter disappointment at Lee's miraculous escape, and had it not been for his success on the field of battle, Meade would undoubtedly have been removed from the chief command. As it was, however, he retained his position and for months he lay comparatively idle, watching his opponent who busied himself with filling the broken ranks of his army for a renewal of the struggle.

Meanwhile, the Confederate newspapers began a bitter criticism of Lee, charging that he had displayed bad judgment and worse generalship in attempting to invade the North. A man of different caliber would, doubtless, have answered these attacks by exposing some of the officers whose conduct was largely responsible for the failure of the campaign. Indeed, the facts would have justified him in dismissing more than one of his subordinates from the army in disgrace, and had he chosen to speak the word he might easily have ruined the reputation of at least one distinguished general.

But no such selfish or vindictive thought ever crossed Lee's mind. Keenly as he suffered from the abuse which was heaped upon him, he endured it without a murmur and, when at last he felt obliged to notice it, his reply took the form of a letter to the Confederate President requesting his permission to resign.

"The general remedy for the want of success in a military commander is his removal," he wrote a month after the battle of Gettysburg. "I do not know how far the expressions of discontent in the public journals extend in the army. My brother officers have been too kind to report it and, so far, the troops have been too generous to exhibit it. I, therefore, beg you to take measures to supply my place, because if I cannot accomplish what I myself desire, how can I fulfill the expectations of others? I must confess, too that my eyesight is not good and that I am so dull that in making use of the eyes of others I am frequently misled. Everything, therefore, points to the advantages to be derived from a new commander. A younger and abler man can readily be obtained--one that would accomplish more than I can perform and all that I have wished. I have no complaints to make of anyone but myself. I have received nothing but kindness from those above me and the most considerate attention from my comrades and companions in arms."

This generous, dignified statement, modest to the point of self-effacement, instantly hushed all discontent and, before it, even the newspaper editors stood abashed.

"Where am I to find the new commander who is to possess that greater ability which you believe to be required?" wrote Jefferson Davis in reply. "If Providence should kindly offer such a person I would not hesitate to avail myself of his services. But my sight is not sufficiently penetrating to discover such hidden merit, if it exists. To ask me to substitute you by someone more fit to command is to demand an impossibility."

In the face of this graceful response Lee could no longer urge his resignation, and after waiting for more than three months for Meade to attack, he suddenly assumed the offensive and during the next five months he and Meade maneuvered their armies as two chess experts handle the pieces on the board. Again and again, Meade swung his powerful army into a favorable position and, again and again, Lee responded with a move which placed his opponent on the defensive.

But while this game of check and countercheck was being played, the North was becoming more and more impatient and events were rapidly bringing another player to the fore.

Chapter XXIV
The Rescue of Two Armies

The defeats and disappointments of the various campaigns in Virginia had gradually convinced the authorities at Washington that too many people were trying to direct the Union forces. With Lee there was practically no interference; but the commanders who opposed him were subject to the orders of the General-in-Chief at Washington, who was, to some extent, controlled by the Secretary of War, whose superior was the President, and after almost every engagement a Congressional Committee, known as the "committee on the conduct of the war," held a solemn investigation in which praise and blame were distributed with the best intentions and worst possible results. All these offices and officials were accordingly more or less responsible for everything that occurred, but not one of them was ever wholly to blame. This mistake, however, was at last fully realized and a careful search began for some one man to whom the supreme command could be entrusted. But for a long time no one apparently thought that the Western army contained any very promising material. Nevertheless, Grant, Sheridan, Sherman and Rosecrans were then in that army and, of these four; Rosecrans was regarded by many as the only real possibility.

Indeed, at the moment when Grant was closing in upon Vicksburg, and Lee and Meade were struggling at Gettysburg, Rosecrans, who had been entrusted with the important duty of conducting a campaign to drive the Confederates out of Tennessee, was fully justifying the high opinions of his admirers. Between June 24, 1863, and September 9th of that year he certainly outmaneuvered his opponents, occupying the all-important position of Chattanooga, and forcing the able Confederate General Bragg to fall back with more speed than order.

During all this time the North had been insisting that the army should be placed in charge of some commander who could master Lee, and this demand had found expression in a popular poem bearing the refrain "Abraham Lincoln! Give us a Man!" To the minds of many people Rosecrans had clearly demonstrated that he was "the Man," and it is possible that his subsequent acts were prompted by over-eagerness to end his already successful campaign with a startlingly brilliant feat of arms. At all events, he determined not to rest satisfied with having driven the Confederates from the field, but to capture or destroy their entire force.

With this idea he divided his army and rushed it by different routes over the mountains in hot pursuit of the foe. But the trouble with this program was that Bragg had not really retreated at all, having merely moved his army aside waiting for an opportunity to strike. Indeed, Rosecrans had barely plunged his troops into the various mountain passes on their fruitless errand before the whole Confederate force loomed up, threatening to destroy his widely-separated, pursuing columns, one by one, before they could be united.

This unexpected turn of affairs utterly unnerved the Union General, and although he did manage by desperate exertions to collect his scattered army, he completely lost his head when Bragg attacked him at Chickamauga, Georgia, on the 19th of September, 1863, and before the savage battle of that name had ended he retired from the field, believing that his army had been totally destroyed.

Such, undoubtedly, would have been its fate had not General Thomas and his brave troops covered the retreat, by holding the whole Confederate army in check for hours and even forcing it to yield portions of the bloody field. From that day forward Thomas was known as "The Rock of Chickamauga," but the heroic stand of his gallant men barely sufficed to save the Union army, which reached the intrenchments of Chattanooga only just in time, with the Confederates hot upon its trail.

Had Bragg overtaken his flying opponent, he would doubtless have made an end of him then and there, but it was not altogether with regret that he saw him enter Chattanooga, for with the roads properly blocked he knew the place would prove a perfect trap. He, accordingly, began a close siege which instantly cut off all Rosecrans' communication with the outside world, except by one road which was in such a wretched condition as to be impossible for a retreating army. Indeed, the heavy autumn rains soon rendered it impracticable even for provision wagons, and as no supplies could reach the army by any other route, it was not long before starvation began to stare the besieged garrison in the face.

Meanwhile, Rosecrans, almost wild with anxiety and mortification, sent dispatch after dispatch to Washington describing his condition and imploring aid, but though he still had an effective army under his command and plenty of ammunition, he made no attempt whatever to save himself from his impending doom. Day by day the situation grew more and more perilous; thousands upon thousands of horses and mules died for lack of food and the men were so nearly reduced to starvation that they greedily devoured the dry corn intended for the animals.

All this time the authorities in Washington were straining every nerve to rescue the beleaguered army. Sixteen thousand men under General Hooker were rushed to its relief, provisions were forwarded within a day's march of the town, awaiting the opening of new roads, and finally, when the stream of frantic telegrams from the front showed that the army had practically no leadership, hurried orders were forwarded to Grant, authorizing him to remove Rosecrans, place Thomas temporarily in control and take the field himself at the earliest possible moment.

This unexpected summons found Grant in a serious condition, for some weeks earlier his horse had fallen under him, crushing his leg so severely that for a time it was feared he might be crippled for life, and he was still on crutches suffering intense pain when the exciting orders were placed in his hands. Nevertheless, he promptly started on his desperate errand, traveling at first by rail and steamer and then in an ambulance, until its jolting motion became unbearable when he had himself lifted into the saddle with the grim determination of riding the remainder of the way. Even for a man in perfect physical condition the journey would have been distressing, for the roads, poor at their best, were knee deep in mud and a wild storm of wind and rain was raging. Time and again his escort had to lift the General from his horse and carry him across dangerous washouts and unaffordable streams, but at the earliest possible moment they were always ordered to swing him into the saddle again.

Thus, mile after mile and hour after hour, the little cavalcade crept toward Chattanooga, Grant's face becoming more haggard and furrowed with pain at every step, but showing a fixed determination to reach his goal at any cost. On every side signs of the desperate plight of the besieged garrison were only too apparent. Thousands of carcasses of starved horses and mules lay beside the road amid broken-down wagons, abandoned provisions and all the wreckage of a disorganized and demoralized army.

But if the suffering officer noted these ominous evidences of disaster, his face afforded no expression of his thought. Plastered with mud and drenched to the skin, he rode steadily forward, speaking no word and scarcely glancing to the right or left, and when at last the excruciating journey came to an end, he hastened to interview Thomas and hear his report, without even waiting to change his clothes or obtain refreshment of any kind.

It was not a very cheerful story which Thomas confided to his Chief before the blazing headquarters' fire, but the dripping and exhausted General listened to it with no indication of discouragement or dismay. "What efforts have been made to open up other roads for provisioning the army?" was the first question, and Thomas showed him a plan which he and Rosecrans had worked out. Grant considered it in silence for a moment and then nodded his approval. The only thing wrong with the plan was that it had not been carried out, was his comment, and after a personal inspection of the lines he gave the necessary authority for putting it into immediate operation. Orders accordingly began flying right and left, and within twenty-four hours the army was busily engaged in gnawing a way out of the trap.

Additional roads were essential for safety but to gain them the Confederates had to be attacked and a heavy force was therefore ordered to seize and hold a point known as Brown's Ferry. This relieved the situation at once and meanwhile the new commander had hurried a special messenger to Sherman, ordering him to drop everything else and march his Vicksburg veterans toward Chattanooga without an instant's delay. The advance of this strong reenforcement was promptly reported to Bragg, who saw at a glance that unless it could be stopped there was every prospect that his Chattanooga victims would escape.

He accordingly determined upon a very bold but very dangerous move. Not far away lay General Burnside and a small Union army, guarding the important city of Knoxville, Tennessee, and against this the Confederate commander dispatched a heavy force, in the hope that Grant would be compelled to send Sherman to the rescue.

But the effect of this news upon Grant was very different from Bragg's expectations, for realizing that his adversary must have seriously weakened himself in sending the expedition against Burnside, he ordered Hooker, whose 16,000 men were already on hand, to make an immediate attack with a force drawn from various parts of the army, and on November 24, 1863, after a fierce engagement known as the battle of Lookout Mountain, the Union troops drove their opponents from one of the two important heights commanding Chattanooga.

In this success Sherman had effectively cooperated by attacking and holding the northern end of Missionary Ridge and Grant determined to follow up his advantage by moving the very next morning against this second and more formidable range of hills. Therefore, ordering Hooker to attack the Confederate right on Missionary Ridge and get in their rear at that point while Sherman assaulted their left, he held Thomas's troops lying in their trenches at the front awaiting a favorable opportunity to send them crashing through the center.

The main field of battle was plainly visible to the silent commander as he looked down upon it from a hill known as Orchard Knob, and he watched the effect of the attacks on both wings of the Confederate line with intense interest. Reenforcements were evidently being hurried to the Confederate right and left and Hooker, delayed by the destruction of a bridge, did not appear at the critical moment. Nevertheless, for some time Sherman continued to advance, but as Grant saw him making slower progress and noted the heavy massing of troops in his path, he ordered Thomas's waiting columns to attack the center and carry the breastworks at the foot of Missionary Ridge.

With a blare of bugles, 20,000 blue-coated men seemed to leap from the ground and 20,000 bayonets pointed at Missionary Ridge whose summits began to blaze forth shot and shell. Death met them at every stride but the charging troops covered the ground between them and the rifle pits they had been ordered to take in one wild rush and tore over them like an angry sea. Then, to the utter astonishment of all beholders, instead of halting, they continued charging up the face of Missionary Ridge, straight into the mouths of the murderous cannon.

"By whose order is this?" Grant demanded sternly.

"By their own, I fancy," answered Thomas.

Incredible as this suggestion seemed, it offered the only possible explanation of the scene. No officer would have dared to order troops to such certain destruction as apparently awaited them on the fire-crowned slopes of Missionary Ridge. Spellbound Grant followed the men as they crept further and further up the height, expecting every instant to see them hurled back as Pickett's heroes were at Gettysburg, when suddenly wave upon wave of blue broke over the crest, the Union flags fluttered all along the line and before this extraordinary charge the Confederates broke and fled in disorder.

Setting spur to his horse, Grant dashed across the hard-fought field and up the formidable ridge, issuing orders for securing all that had been gained. An opening wedge had now been inserted in Chattanooga's prison doors, and by midnight the silent captain had thrown his whole weight against them and they fell. Then calmly turning his attention to Burnside, he ordered him to hold his position at every hazard until he could come to the rescue and, setting part of his victorious veterans in motion toward Knoxville, soon relieved its garrison from all danger.

With the rescue of two Union armies to his credit Grant was generally regarded as the most fitting candidate for the chief command of the army, but by this time it was fully realized that the man who held that position would have to be invested with far greater powers than any Union general had thus far possessed. Halleck expressed himself as only too anxious to resign; Congress passed a law reviving the grade of lieutenant-general with powers which, up to that time, had never been entrusted to anyone save Washington, and responded to the cry, "Abraham Lincoln! Give us a MAN!" the President, on March 1st, 1864, nominated Ulysses Grant as Commander-in-Chief of all the armies of the United States.

Chapter XXV
Lieutenant-General Grant

Until he arrived in Washington Lincoln had never met the man to whom he had entrusted the supreme command of the army, and the new General was a very different individual from those who had been previously appointed to high rank. Some of his predecessors had possessed undoubted ability, but most of them had soon acquired an exaggerated idea of their own importance, surrounding themselves with showy staffs in gorgeous attire, delighting in military pomp and etiquette of every kind, and generally displaying a great weakness for popular admiration and applause. Moreover, all of them, with the exception of Meade, had talked too much for their own good and that of the army, so that many of their plans had become known in Richmond almost as soon as they had been formed. Indeed, they not only talked, but wrote too much, and in discussions with their superiors and wrangling with their fellow officers more than one proved far mightier with the pen than with the sword. All this, to a very large extent, was the fault of the public, for it had made an idol of each new General, deluging him with praise, flattering his vanity and fawning on him until he came to regard the war as a sort of background for his own greatness. Thus, for almost three years, the war was conducted more like a great game than a grim business, and not until it began visibly to sap the life blood and resources of the nation did the people, as a whole, realize the awful task confronting them.

Both sides had begun the conflict in much the same careless fashion, but the South had immediately become the battle ground, and the horrors of war actually seen and felt by its people quickly sobered even the most irresponsible. But from the very first Lee had taken a serious view of the whole situation. Every word he spoke or wrote concerning it was distinctly tinged with solemnity, if not sadness, and his sense of responsibility had a marked influence upon the whole Confederacy. It had taken the North almost three years to respond in a similar spirit, but by that time it was ready for a leader who knew what war really meant and for whom it had no glory, and such a leader had undoubtedly been found in Grant.

In the evening of March 8, 1864, the new commander arrived in Washington and made his way, without attracting any attention, to one of the hotels. There was nothing in his presence or manner to indicate that he was a person of any importance. Indeed, he presented a decidedly commonplace appearance, for he walked with an awkward lurch and bore himself in a slouchy fashion which made him even shorter than he was. Moreover, his uniform was faded and travel-stained, his close-cropped beard and hair were unkempt, and his attire was careless to the point of slovenliness. There was, however, something in the man's clear-cut features, firm mouth and chin and resolute blue eyes which suggested strength, and while his face, as a whole, would not have attracted any particular notice in a crowd, no one in glancing at it would have been inclined to take any liberties with its owner.

But though Grant had arrived unheralded and unrecognized at the national capital, he had barely given his name to the hotel clerk before the whole city was surging about him eager to catch a glimpse of the new hero and cheer him to the echo. But however much notoriety of this sort had pleased some of his predecessors, Grant soon showed that he wanted no applauding mob to greet him in the streets, for he quickly escaped to the seclusion of his own room. But the same public that had cheered itself hoarse for McClellan, Pope and Hooker, and then hissed them all in turn, had found another hero and was not to be cheated of its prey. Indeed, the newcomer was not even allowed to eat his dinner in peace, for a crowd of gaping and congratulating enthusiasts descended upon him the moment he reappeared and soon drove him from the dining room in sheer disgust.

Possibly the fate of the fallen idols had warned Grant against making a public exhibition of himself or encouraging the hysterical acclamations of the crowd, but he was naturally a man of sound, common sense, entirely free from conceit, and he had no idea of allowing the idle or curious mob to amuse itself at his expense. He, therefore, quickly made it plain that he had serious work to do and that he intended to do it without nonsense of any kind.

Ceremonies and forms with such a man would have been impossible, and on

March 9, 1864, President Lincoln handed him his commission as a Lieutenant-General, with a few earnest words to which he made a modest reply, and then, with the same calmness he had displayed in assuming the colonelcy of the 21st Illinois, he turned to the duties involved in the command of half a million men.

From that time forward no more councils of war were held at the White House and no more military secrets were disclosed to the Confederate chiefs. "I do not know General Grant's plans, and I do not want to know them!" exclaimed Lincoln with relief. But other people did want to know them and the newspaper reporters and busybodies of all sorts incessantly buzzed about him, employing every device from subtle flattery to masked threats to discover his designs. But Grant knew "how to keep silent in seven different languages" and no one could beguile him into opening his lips. Neither had he time nor inclination to listen to other people talk. His troops were spread over a thousand miles of territory, and never before had they been under the absolute control of any one man. With the Army of the Potomac he had had but little practical experience; of the country in which its campaigns had been conducted he knew nothing at first hand; with a few exceptions he had no personal acquaintance with the officers under his immediate command, and there were countless other difficulties which had to be overcome. He, therefore, had no leisure for trifling and quickly sent all intruders about their business while he attended to his own.

The problem involved in a grand campaign was in many respects new to him, but doing his own thinking in silence, instead of puzzling himself with the contradictory opinions of other men, Grant reached a more accurate conclusion in regard to the war than any of his predecessors. In the first place, he saw that the various campaigns which had been conducted in different parts of the country would have been far more effective had they all formed part of one plan enabling the different armies to cooperate with each other. He, accordingly, determined to conduct the war on a gigantic scale, keeping the Confederates in the West so busy that they would not be able to reenforce Lee and giving Lee no chance to help them. In a word, he intended to substitute team play for individual effort all along the line.

Again, he saw the capture of Richmond, upon which the Army of the Potomac had expended all its efforts, would be futile if Lee's army remained undefeated in the field, and he resolved that Lee and not Richmond should thereafter be the main object of the campaign. "Where Lee's army goes, there you will go also," was the substance of his first order to Meade who virtually became his Chief of Staff, and those who were straining every nerve to discover his plan and expecting something very brilliant or subtle never guessed that those nine words contained the open secret of his whole campaign.

Such, however, was the fact. "I never maneuver," he remarked to his Chief of Staff; and Meade, who had spent the best part of a year in a great series of maneuvers with Lee, listened to this confession with astonishment and dismay, scarcely believing that his superior really meant what he said. But Grant did mean it. No elaborate moves or delicate strategy had been employed in any of his campaigns and he had yet to meet with a serious defeat. To make his first experiment in maneuvering against such an expert in the science of war as Lee, would have been to foredoom himself to defeat. With a far smaller force then either McClellan, Pope, Burnside, Hooker or Meade had possessed, the Confederate leader had practically fought a drawn battle with them for three years. His science had not, it is true, been able to overcome their numbers, but their numbers had not overpowered him. This, as far as anyone could see, might go on forever.

But Grant knew that the North had long been tiring of the war and that unless it were speedily closed the Union might be sacrificed in order to obtain peace. Moreover, he saw that every day the war lasted cost an enormous sum of money, and that the loss of life on the battle field was nothing compared to that in the hospitals and prisons, where disease and starvation were claiming scores of victims every hour.

He, therefore, determined to fight and continue fighting until he pounded his opponent to pieces, well knowing that almost every able-bodied man in the South was already in the army and that there was practically no one left to take the place of those who fell.

This policy, in the minds of many people, proves that Grant was no general, but merely a brute and a butcher. But history has never yet revealed a military leader who, having the advantage of numbers, did not make the most of it. Had Grant been waging war for war's sake, or been so enamored with his profession as to care more for its fine points than for the success of his cause, he might have evolved some more subtle and less brutal plan. But he had no love for soldiering and no sentimental ideas whatever about the war. Common sense, with which he was liberally supplied, told him that the only excuse for fighting was to uphold principles which were vital to the national life and the only way to have those principles upheld was to defeat those who opposed them and to do this he determined to use all the resources at his command.

The two men whom Fate or Chance had been drawing together for over two hundred years were utterly different in appearance and manner, but in other respects they were singularly alike. Lee was, at the time of their meeting, already in his 58th year, his hair and beard were almost white, but his calm, handsome face, clear eyes and ruddy complexion, made him appear younger than he was. His bearing also was that of a young man, for his erect, soldierly carriage showed his height to full advantage; his well-knit figure was almost slight for a man standing over six feet, and, mounted on his favorite horse "Traveller," he was the ideal soldier. Grant was barely forty-two years of age, short of stature, careless in dress and generally indifferent to appearances. His face, though strong, was somewhat coarse, his manners were not polished and he had nothing of the cultivation or charm which Lee so unmistakably possessed.

But though Grant thus reflected his Roundhead ancestors and Lee his Cavalier descent, the contrast between them was mainly external. Both were modest and courageous; both were self-contained; each had his tongue and temper under complete control; each was essentially an American in his ideas and ideals; each fought for a principle in which he sincerely believed, and neither took the least delight in war. Had they met in times of peace, it is not probable that they would have become intimate friends, but it is certain that each would have respected, if not admired the other for his fine qualities, and this was undoubtedly their attitude toward each other from the beginning of the struggle.

Chapter XXVI
A Duel to the Death

For nearly two months after Grant assumed command no important move was attempted by either the Union or the Confederate forces except in Mississippi. Both sides realized that a desperate struggle was impending and each needed all the time it could gain to prepare for the coming fray. Heavy reenforcements were hurried to Grant, until the Army of the Potomac under his immediate command included over 120,000 men; a hundred thousand more were assembled at Chattanooga in charge of Sherman; and two other forces of considerable size were formed to cooperate with Grant--one being entrusted to General Benjamin Butler and the other to General Franz Sigel.

To oppose this vast army Lee had less than 65,000 men in the Army of Northern Virginia and the only other formidable Confederate force in the field was that commanded by General Joseph Johnston, who, with some 53,000 men, was stationed in Georgia guarding the cotton states and the far South. If these two armies could be captured or destroyed, all organized resistance to the Union would be at an end, and Grant, accordingly, determined to throw his entire weight upon them, sending Sherman against Johnston, Butler against the City of Richmond and Sigel against the rich Shenandoah Valley which supplied the Confederate armies with food, while he himself attacked Lee with an overwhelming force.

Never before had a Union general undertaken a campaign covering such a vast extent of country and never before had such a united effort been made to exhaust the armies and the resources of the South. With his own forces threatened by superior numbers Lee would not be able to reenforce Johnston with safety and, confronted by Sherman, Johnston would find it impossible to send assistance to Lee. This promised to bring the war to a speedy close, and the supporters of the Union redoubled their praises of the Lieutenant-General as they began to understand his plan. Indeed, the more he avoided publicity and applause and the more indifference he showed for popular opinion, the more the newspapers and the general public fawned upon him, and when, on May 3, 1864, he ordered his armies to advance, the whole North was fairly aflame with enthusiasm.

It was certainly a momentous occasion. Three years earlier Grant had been utterly unknown to the country at large and the small group who acknowledged his acquaintance had regarded him as a rather pitiful failure, while the Government to whom he had offered his services had ignored him altogether. Now, at his nod, hundreds of thousands of men instantly sprang to arms and the most powerful armies that America had ever seen moved forward in obedience to his will, Sherman marching southward, Butler creeping toward Richmond, Sigel advancing into the fertile Shenandoah Valley, and the Army of the Potomac crossing the Rapidan River to renew its struggle with Lee.

Lee had watched the elaborate preparations of his new antagonist with keen interest and no little apprehension, for Grant's record as a fighting man promised a duel to the death and the South had no more men.

The situation was certainly serious but, anxious as he was, the Confederate commander did not by any means despair. He was familiar with every inch of the country through which Grant would have to advance and the chances were that this would, sooner or later, give him not only the advantage of position, but possibly the choice of weapons. With this idea he allowed the Union forces to cross the Rapidan unopposed, hoping that he would soon be able to drive them back and that the river would then be as valuable as cavalry in hampering their retreat. Just beyond the Rapidan lay the dense thickets and waste lands of scrub oak and undergrowth known as the Wilderness, which had witnessed the Chancellorsville surprise and virtually sealed the fate of Hooker's army. If the Union forces advanced directly through this jungle, there was more than a possibility that they might outflank their opponents and gain the road to Richmond, but Lee scarcely dared hope that his adversary would attempt so dangerous a route. Nevertheless, he maneuvered to leave the trap undisturbed, and when he saw the Union columns entering the forests he felt that they were actually being delivered into his hands. Once in those tangled thickets he knew that Grant's artillery and cavalry would be practically useless and without them his superiority in numbers disappeared. Of course, it would be impossible to conduct a scientific battle in such a region, for it would virtually be fighting in the dark, but knowing that his men were thoroughly familiar with the ground, Lee determined to hurl them upon the advancing blue-coats, trusting to the gloom and the terrors of the unknown to create confusion and panic in their ranks.

But the men whom Grant commanded were no longer the inexperienced volunteers who had been stampeded at Bull Run. They were veterans of many campaigns and, though they staggered for a moment under the shock of battle, they speedily rallied and fought with stubborn courage. The conflict that followed was one of the most brutal recorded in the annals of modern war. Whole regiments sprang at each other's throats, the men fighting each other like animals; trees were cut down by the bullets which tore through them from every direction; bursting shells set fire to the woods, suffocating the wounded or burning them to death; wild charges were made, ending in wilder stampedes or bloody repulses; the crackle of flames rose high above the pandemonium of battle and dense smoke-clouds drifted chokingly above this hideous carnival of death. Thus for two days the armies staggered backward and forward with no result save a horrible loss of life. Once the Union forces almost succeeded in gaining a position which would have disposed of their adversaries, but Lee saw the danger just in the nick of time and, rushing a Texas brigade to the rescue, led the charge in person until his troops recognized him and forced him to retire.

It was May 7, 1864, when this blind slaughter known as the Battle of the Wilderness ceased, but by that time nearly 18,000 Union soldiers and 12,000 Confederates lay upon the field. Lee could not claim a victory but he still held his ground and he felt confident that Grant would fall back behind the Rapidan River to recuperate his shattered forces. No Union commander, thus far, had tarried long on Virginian soil after such a baptism of blood, and when the news that Grant's columns were retreating reached the Confederate commander he breathed a sigh of thanksgiving and relief.

To the veterans who had served under McClellan, Pope, Burnside and Hooker, retreats were a wretchedly familiar experience, but they had not been long on the road before they realized that they were not retreating but were marching southward. As the truth of this dawned upon the disheartened columns they burst into frantic cheers for Grant and pressed forward with springy steps, shouting and singing for joy.

A less able commander would have been fatally misled by Grant's apparent retreat, but Lee knew that he might again attempt to swing around his right flank and edge toward Richmond by way of Spotsylvania, and to guard against this a body of troops had been ordered to block that road. Therefore, by the time Grant began his great turning movement, Lee was planted squarely across his path and another series of battles followed. Here the Union commander was able to make some use of his cavalry and artillery, but the Confederates offset this by fighting behind intrenchments and they repulsed charge after charge with fearful slaughter. Again, as at the Battle of the Wilderness, the gray line was pierced, this time at a point known as the "Bloody Angle" or "Hell's Half Acre," and twice Lee sprang forward to lead a desperate charge to recover the lost ground. But each time the troops refused to advance until their beloved leader retired to a point of safety, and when he yielded they whirled forward, sweeping everything before them.

These charges saved the battle of Spotsylvania for the Confederates. But though Lee had again blocked his opponent, the fact that he had thrice had to rally his troops at the peril of his life showed that he had been harder pressed than in any of his other Virginia campaigns. Nevertheless, when the last furious attack had been repulsed and Grant began moving sullenly away, it seemed as though he had at last been compelled to abandon the campaign. But the wearied Confederates had yet to learn that their terrible opponent was a man who did not know when he was beaten, for in spite of his awful losses he had written his government May 11, 1864, "I propose to fight it out on this line if it takes all summer," and his army, instead of retreating, continued to move southward, crossing the North Anna River and circling once more toward the left flank.

Again Grant was on the road to Richmond, but in crossing the North Anna River he left an opening between the two wings of his army and before he could close it Lee threw his whole force into the breach and, completely cutting off one part of the Union army from the other, held both firmly in check. This masterly move might have brought Grant's campaign to a disastrous end, but just as he was planning to take full advantage of it, Lee fell ill and during his absence from the field Grant made his first backward move, recrossing the North Anna River and, bringing the two wings of his army together, rescued it from its perilous position.

The moment he reached a point of safety, however, the persistent commander recommenced his march by the left flank, sidling once more toward Richmond until he reached Cold Harbor, only eight miles from the Confederate capital. Here Lee once more interposed his battered forces, strongly intrenching them in a position that fairly defied attack. With any other adversary against him he would have concluded that the game was won, for by all the rules of war the Union army was completely balked and could not avoid a retreat. But Grant was a man of a different caliber from any he had encountered heretofore. In spite of checks and disasters and unheard-of slaughter he had pushed inexorably forward; foiled in front he had merely turned aside to hew another bloody path. To him defeat only seemed to mean delay, and apparently he could not be shaken from his dogged purpose, no matter what the cost. At Cold Harbor, however, the Confederate position was so strong that to assault it was madness, and Lee could not believe that even his grim opponent would resort to such a suicidal attempt. But retreat or attack offered no choice to Grant's mind, and on June 2, 1864, the troops were fiercely hurled against the Confederate works, only to be repulsed with fearful slaughter. A few hours later orders were issued to renew the assault, and then postponed for a day.

That delay gave the soldiers an opportunity to understand the desperate nature of the work that lay before them and, realizing that charging against murderous batteries and trenches meant rushing into the jaws of death, they offered a silent protest. Not a man refused to obey orders, not one fell from his place in the line, but to their coats they sewed strips of cloth bearing their names and addresses so that their bodies might be identified upon the field.

This dramatic spectacle might well have warned their commander of the hopelessness of his attempt, but fixed in his resolve to thrust his opponent from his path, he gave the fatal order to charge, and twenty minutes later 3,000 of his best troops fell before the smoking trenches and the balance reeled back aghast at the useless sacrifice. This horrifying slaughter, which Grant himself confessed was a grievous blunder, brought the first stage of his campaign to a close. In but little over a month he had lost nearly 55,000 men--almost as many as Lee had had in his entire army, and almost in sight of the spires of Richmond his adversary held him securely at arm's length.

A wave of horror, indignation and disappointment, swept over the North. Another campaign had proved a failure. There were, however, two men who did not agree with this conclusion. One was Grant, pouring over the maps showing the movements of all his armies. The other was Lee, looking in vain for reenforcements to fill the gaps in his fast thinning lines.

Chapter XXVII
Check and Countercheck

The six-weeks' campaign in Virginia had been quite sufficient to check all enthusiasm for Grant, but the fact that he was no longer a popular hero did not trouble him at all. Indeed, he displayed the same indifference to the storm of angry criticism that he had shown for the salvos of applause. He had made no claims or boasts before he took the field and he returned no answers to the accusations and complaints after his apparent failures. Had he posed before the public as a hero or been tempted to prophesy a speedy triumph for his army, the humiliation and disappointment might have driven him to resign from the command. But he had recognized the difficulty of his task from the outset, modestly accepting it with no promise save that he would do his best, and he silently resolved to pursue the campaign he had originally mapped out in spite of all reverses.

Certainly, he required all his calmness and steadfastness to overcome his discouragement and disgust at the manner in which the cooperating armies had been handled. In the Shenandoah Valley Sigel had proved utterly incompetent and the Confederates, instead of having been driven from that important storehouse, had tightened their hold upon it. Moreover, Butler, who was supposed to threaten Richmond while Grant fought Lee, had made a sorry mess of that part of the program. In fact he had maneuvered in such a ridiculous fashion that he and about 35,000 troops were soon cooped up by a far smaller force of Confederates who held them as a cork holds the contents of a bottle; and last, but not least, the Army of Potomac lay badly mutilated before the impassable intrenchments of Lee.

In one particular, however, Grant's expectations bade fair to be realized, for Sherman was steadily pushing his way through Georgia, driving Johnston before him, and inflicting terrible damage upon the country through which he passed. As

Grant watched this triumphant advance he silently resolved upon another move. The north or front door of Richmond was closed and firmly barred. There was nothing to be gained by further battering at that portal. But the southern or rear door had not yet been thoroughly tried and upon that he concluded to make a determined assault. To do this it would be necessary to renew his movement around his opponent's right flank by crossing the formidable James River--a difficult feat at any time, but double difficult at that moment, owing to the fact that Butler's "bottled" force might be crushed by a Confederate attack while the hazardous passage of the river was being effected. Nevertheless, he decided to risk this bold stroke, and during the night of June 12, 1864, about ten days after the repulse at Cold Harbor, the great movement was begun.

Meanwhile Lee, confident that he had completely checked his opponent, but disappointed that he had not forced him to retreat, determined to drive him away by carrying the war into the North and threatening the Federal capital. That he should have been able to attempt this in the midst of a campaign deliberately planned to destroy him, affords some of the indication of the brilliant generalship he had displayed. But it does not fully reflect his masterful daring. At the outset of the campaign the Union forces had outnumbered him two to one and its losses had been offset by reenforcements, while every man that had fallen in the Confederate ranks had left an empty space. It is highly probable, therefore, that at the moment he resolved to turn the tables on his adversary and transform the campaign against Richmond into a campaign against Washington, he had not much more than one man to his opponent's three. Nevertheless, in the face of these overwhelming numbers, he maintained a bold front towards Grant and detached General Jubal Early with 20,000 men to the Shenandoah Valley, with orders to clear that region of Union troops, cross the Potomac River and then march straight on Washington.

It was at this moment that Grant began creeping cautiously away toward the rear door of Richmond. To keep a vigilant enemy in entire ignorance of such a tremendous move was, of course, impossible, but the system and discipline which he had instilled into his army almost accomplished the feat. Indeed, so rapidly and silently did the troops move, so perfect were the arrangements for transporting their baggage and supplies, so completely were the details of the whole undertaking ordered and systematized, that over a hundred thousand men, infantry, cavalry, and artillery, with their horses, hospital and wagon trains, and all the paraphernalia of a vast army virtually faded away, and when Lee gazed from his intrenchments on June 13, 1864, there was no sign of his opponent and he did not discover where he had gone for fully four days.

In the meantime, Grant had thrown his entire army across the James River and was advancing, horse and foot, on Petersburg, the key to the approach to Richmond from the south, and Butler, whose troops had been extricated from their difficulties, was ordered to seize it. Petersburg was at that moment wholly unprepared to resist a strong attack. Indeed, there were only a handful of men guarding the fortification, the capture of which would case the fall of Richmond, but Butler was not the man to take advantage of this great opportunity. On the contrary, he delayed his advance and otherwise displayed such wretched judgment that the Confederates had time to rush reenforcements to the rescue, and when Grant arrived on the scene the intrenchments were strongly occupied. Notwithstanding this the Union commander ordered a vigorous assault, and for three days the troops were hurled against the breastworks without result. The last attack was made on June 18, 1864, but by this time 10,000 Union soldiers had been sacrificed and Lee had arrived in person with strong support. Grant accordingly, abandoning his efforts to carry the place by storm, began to close in upon it for a grimly sullen siege.

Meanwhile, General Early, to whom Lee had entrusted his counter-move, was sweeping away the Federal forces in the Shenandoah Valley with resistless fury, and suddenly, to the intense surprise and mortification of the whole North, advanced upon Washington, threatening it with capture. Washington was almost as completely unprepared for resistance as Petersburg had been, its defenses being manned by only a small force mainly composed of raw recruits and invalid soldiers, while outside the city there was but one body of troops near enough to oppose the Confederate advance. That little army, however, was commanded by General Lew Wallace, later the famous author of "Ben Hur," and he had the intelligence to see that he might at least delay Early by offering battle and that gaining time might prove as valuable as gaining a victory. Accordingly, he threw himself across the Confederate's path and, though roughly handled and at last driven from the field, he hung on long enough to accomplish his purpose and although his adversary attempted to make up for lost time by rapid marching he did not succeed. This undoubtedly saved Washington from capture, for shortly after Early appeared on the 7th Street Road leading to the capital, the reenforcements which Grant had rushed forward reached the city, and before any attack on the intrenchments was attempted they were fully defended and practically unassailable. Seeing this, Early retreated with the Union troops following in half-hearted pursuit.

It was the 12th of July, 1864, when, with a sigh of intense relief, Washington saw the backs of the retreating Confederates, but its satisfaction at its escape was mingled with indignation against Grant for having left it open to attack. Indeed, he was regarded by many people as the greatest failure of all the Union commanders, for he had lost more men in sixty days than McClellan had lost in all his campaigns without getting any nearer to Richmond, and by the end of July another lamentable failure was recorded against him.

In the intrenchments facing Petersburg lay the 48th Pennsylvania Volunteers, largely composed of miners from the coal regions of that state. Late in June Colonel Pleasants of this regiment had submitted a plan whereby his men were to dig a tunnel to a point directly under one of the Confederate forts, plant a gunpowder mine there and blow a breach in the defenses through which troops could be poured and the town carried by assault. The scheme was plausible, provided the tunnel could be bored and Grant gave his consent, with the result that within a month an underground passage over 500 feet long was completed, a mine was planted with four tons of powder and elaborate preparations made for storming the Confederate works. Grant's orders were that all obstructions in front of the Union lines should be removed to enable the troops to charge the moment the explosion occurred, and that they should be rushed forward without delay until they were all within the Confederate lines. Accordingly, in the dead of night on July 29th, the assaulting columns were moved into position and when everything was in apparent readiness the signal was given to explode the mine. But though the match was applied no explosion occurred, and in the awful hush that followed Lieut. Jacob Douty and Sergeant Henry Rees volunteered to crawl into the tunnel and see what was wrong. To enter the passage at that moment was almost defying death, but the two men took their lives in their hands and, creeping in, discovered that the fuse had smoldered and gone out. They then relit it and made their escape just as a fearful explosion rent the air and great masses of earth, stones and timbers, intermingled with human bodies, leaped toward the sky.

For a moment the waiting troops watched this terrifying spectacle and then, as the cloud of wreckage apparently swerved toward them threatening to descend and bury them beneath it, they fell back in great confusion and some time elapsed before order was restored and the charge begun. But Grant's orders to clear their path had not been obeyed, and the charging troops had to climb over their own breastworks, causing more delay and confusion. Finally, however, the leading brigades reached the great excavation torn by the mine, and there they halted awaiting further orders. But no orders came, for their terror-stricken commander had sought safety in a bomb-proof and when his hiding place was discovered the miserable cur merely mumbled something about "moving forward" and remained cowering in his refuge. Meanwhile, other regiments rushed forward, tumbling in upon one another, until the chasm was choked with men upon whom the Confederates began to pour shot, shell and canister. From that moment everything was lost and at last orders came from Grant to rescue the struggling mass of men from the awful death trap into which they had been plunged, but despite all exertions fully 4,000 were killed, wounded or captured.

Again his subordinates had blundered terribly but Grant accepted the responsibility and assumed the blame, waiting patiently for the hour, then near at hand, when he would find commanders he could trust to carry out his plans.

Chapter XXVIII
The Beginning of the End

The right man to conduct the Shenandoah campaign was already in the Army of the Potomac, but it was not until about a week after the failure of the Petersburg mine that circumstances enabled Grant to place General Philip Sheridan in charge of that important task.

Sheridan, like Sherman, had served with Grant in the West and had developed into a brilliant cavalry leader. Indeed, he was the only man in the Northern armies whose record could be compared with that of Jeb Stuart and many other great cavalry commanders in the South. But Grant felt that Sheridan could handle an entire army as well as he had handled the cavalry alone and he soon showed himself fully worthy of this confidence, for from the moment he took over the command of the Union forces in the Shenandoah Valley, the Confederates were compelled to fight for it as they had never fought before.

Up to this time, the war had been conducted with comparatively little destruction of private property on either side. But the moment had now arrived for harsher measures, for Sherman had occupied Atlanta on September 2, 1864, and was preparing to march to the sea coast and cut the Confederacy in two. If Grant's plan of depriving Lee of the fertile valley to the north was to be put in operation, there was no time to lose. Sheridan, accordingly, at once proceeded to attack the Confederates with the utmost vigor, defeating them in two engagements at Winchester and Fisher's Hill, and following up this success by laying waste the fields and ruthlessly destroying all the stores of grain and provisions which might prove useful to Lee's army. For a month or more he continued to sweep through the country practically unchecked. But on October 19.1864, during his absence, his army was surprised and furiously attacked by General Early's men at Cedar Creek, and before long they had the Union troops in a perilous position which threatened to end in their destruction and the recapture of the entire valley.

Sheridan was at Winchester on his way to the front from Washington when the news of this impending disaster reached him and, mounting his horse, he dashed straight across country for the scene of action. He was then, however, fully twenty miles from the field and there seemed but little chance of his reaching it any time to be of any service. Nevertheless, he spurred forward at a breakneck pace and his splendid horse, responding gamely, fairly flew over the ground, racing along mile after mile at killing speed in a lather of foam and sweat, until the battle field was reached just as the Union troops came reeling back, panic-stricken, under cover of a thin line of troops who had at last succeeded in making a stand.

Instantly, the General was among the fugitives ordering them to turn and follow him and inspired by his presence, they wheeled as he dashed down their broken lines and, madly cheering, hurled themselves upon their pursuers. Completely surprised by this unexpected recovery, the Confederates faltered and the Union troops, gathering force as they charged, rolled them back with irresistible fury and finally swept them completely from the field. Indeed, Early's force was so badly shattered and scattered by this overwhelming defeat that it virtually abandoned the Valley and Sheridan continued his work of destruction almost unopposed, until the whole region was so barren that, as he reported, a crow flying across it would have to carry his own provisions or starve to death.

Meanwhile, Sherman had begun to march from Atlanta to Savannah, Georgia, where he intended to get in touch with the navy guarding the coast and then sweep northward to Grant. Behind him lay the Confederate army, formerly commanded by General Joseph Johnston but now led by General Hood, a daring officer who was expected to retrieve Johnston's failure by some brilliant feat of arms. Whether he would attempt this by following Sherman and attacking him at the first favorable moment or take advantage of his departure to turn north and play havoc with Tennessee and the region thus exposed to attack, was uncertain. To meet either of these moves Sherman sent a substantial part of his army to General Thomas at Nashville, Tennessee, and swung off with the rest of his troops toward the sea. Hood instantly advanced against Thomas, and Grant at Petersburg, closely watching the movement saw a great opportunity to dispose of one of the Confederate armies. He, accordingly, ordered Thomas to attack with his whole strength as soon as Hood reached Nashville, but although the Confederates reached that point considerably weakened by a partial defeat inflicted on them by a retreating Union column, Thomas delayed his assault. Days of anxious waiting followed and then Grant hurried General Logan, one of his most trusted officers, to the scene of action with orders to take over the command, unless Thomas immediately obeyed his instructions. In the meantime, however, Thomas, slow but sure, had completed his preparations and, hurling himself upon Hood with a vastly superior force, pursued his retreating columns (Dec. 16, 1864) until they were split into fragments, never again to be reunited as a fighting force.

It was not until this practical annihilation of Hood that the North began to realize how far reaching and complete Grant's plans were. But that event and the Shenandoah campaign made it clear that he had determined that no army worthy of the name should be left to the Confederacy when he finally closed in upon Lee, so that with his destruction or surrender there should be no excuse for prolonging the war. It was in furtherance of this plan that Sherman left ruin and desolation behind him as he blazed his way up from the South. The inhabitants of the region through which he was marching had, up to this time, been living in perfect security and Sherman intended to make war so hideous that they would have no desire to prolong the contest. He, accordingly, tore up the railroads, heating the rails and then twisting them about trees so that they could never be used again, burned public buildings and private dwellings, allowed his army to live on whatever food they could find in the houses, stores or barns, and generally made it a terror to all who lay in the broad path he was sweeping towards Petersburg.

Grant then had Lee fairly caught. His only possible chances of prolonging the contest lay in taking refuge in the mountains or joining his forces with the remnants of Hood's army which had been gathered together and again entrusted with other troops to the command of General Joseph Johnston. Had it been possible to do this, nothing practical would have been achieved, for he had less than 30,000 effective men and Johnston's whole force did not amount to much more than 30,000, while Grant, Sherman and Sheridan together had a quarter of a million men under arms. From a military standpoint Lee knew that the situation was hopeless, but until the authorities who had placed him in the field gave up the cause he felt in duty bound to continue the fight to the bitter end. Had the Union army been his only opponent, it is possible that he might have succeeded in escaping the rings of steel which Grant was daily riveting around him. But he had to fight hunger, and from the day that Sheridan mastered the Shenandoah Valley and Sherman cut off all supplies from the South starvation stared him in the face.

Meanwhile, his troops, though almost reduced to skeletons and clothed in rags, confidently believed that in spite of everything he would find some way of leading them out of Grant's clutches and, inspired by this implicit faith, they hurled themselves again and again upon the masses of troops which were steadily closing around them. But though they frequently checked the advancing columns and sometimes even threw them back, inflicting heavy losses and taking many prisoners, the blue lines soon crept forward again, closing up gap after gap with a resistless tide of men. At last the road to the west leading toward the mountains beyond Lynchburg alone remained open. But to avail himself of this Lee knew that he would have to abandon Petersburg and Richmond and he hesitated to take this step; while Grant, seeing the opening and fearing that his opponent would take advantage of it, strained every nerve to get his troops into a position where they could block the road.

Such was the condition of affairs at the end of March, 1865, but neither the starving soldiers in the Confederate trenches nor the people of Richmond or Petersburg imagined that the end was desperately near. While "Marse Robert," as Lee's men affectionately called him, was in command they felt that no real danger could come nigh them, and their idol was outwardly as calm as in the hour of his greatest triumph.

Chapter XXIX
At Bay

It would be impossible to imagine a more hopeless situation than that which had confronted Lee for many months. To guard the line of intrenchments stretching around Petersburg and Richmond for more than thirty-five miles, he had less than 30,000 effective men, and starvation and disease were daily thinning their impoverished ranks; the soldiers were resorting to the corn intended for the horses, and the cavalry were obliged to disperse through the country seeking fodder for their animals in the wasted fields; the defenders of the trenches, barefooted and in rags, lay exposed to the cold and wet, day and night; there were no medicines for the sick and no great supply of ammunition for the guns.

Perhaps no one but Lee fully realized to what desperate straits his army had been reduced. Certainly his opponents were ignorant of the real condition of affairs or they would have smashed his feeble defenses at a blow, and the fact that he held over a hundred thousand troops at bay for months with a skeleton army shows how skillfully he placed his men.

But though his brilliant career threatened to end in defeat and disaster, no thought of himself ever crossed Lee's mind. Regardless of his own comfort and convenience, he devoted himself day and night to relieving the suffering of his men, who jestingly called themselves "Lee's Miserables," but grimly stuck to their posts with unshaken faith in their beloved chief who, in the midst of confusion and helplessness, remained calm and resourceful, never displaying irritation, never blaming anyone for mistakes, but courageously attempting to make the best of everything and finding time, in spite of all distractions, for the courtesy and the thoughtfulness of a gentleman unafraid.

His letters to his wife and children during these perilous days reveal no anxiety save for the comfort of his men, and no haste except to provide for their wants. At home his wife--confined to an invalid's chair--was busily knitting socks for the soldiers, and to her he wrote in the face of impending disaster:

..."After sending my note this morning I received from the express office a bag of socks. You will have to send down your offerings as soon as you can, and bring your work to a close, for I think General Grant will move against us soon--within a week if nothing prevents--and no man can tell what will be the result; but trusting to a merciful God, who does not always give the battle to the strong, I pray we may not be overwhelmed. I shall, however, endeavor to do my duty and fight to the last. Should it be necessary to abandon our position to prevent being surrounded, what will you do? You must consider the question and make up your mind. It is a fearful condition and we must rely for guidance and protection upon a kind Providence...."

Shortly after this letter was written Lee made a desperate effort to force his adversary to loosen his grip but though the exhausted and starved troops attacked with splendid courage, they could not pierce the solid walls of infantry and fell back with heavy losses. Then Sheridan, who had been steadily closing in from the Shenandoah, swung 10,000 sabres into position and the fate of Petersburg was practically sealed. But, face to face with this calamity, Lee calmly wrote his wife:

"I have received your note with a bag of socks. I return the bag and receipt. I have put in the bag General Scott's autobiography which I thought you might like to read. The General, of course, stands out prominently and does not hide his light under a bushel, but he appears the bold, sagacious, truthful man that he is. I enclose a note from little Agnes. I shall be very glad to see her to-morrow but cannot recommend pleasure trips now...."

At every point Grant was tightening his hold upon the imprisoned garrison and difficulties were crowding fast upon their commander, but he exhibited neither excitement nor alarm. Bending all his energies upon preparations for a retreat, he carefully considered the best plan for moving his troops and supplying their needs on the march, quietly giving his orders to meet emergencies, but allowing no one to see even a shadow of despair on his face. Concerning the gravity of the situation he neither deceived himself nor attempted to deceive others who were entitled to know it, and with absolute accuracy he prophesied the movements of his adversary long before they were made.

...."You may expect Sheridan to move up the Valley," he wrote the Confederate Secretary of War.... "Grant, I think, is now preparing to draw out by his left with the intent of enveloping me. He may wait till his other columns approach nearer, or he may be preparing to anticipate my withdrawal. I cannot tell yet.... Everything of value should be removed from Richmond. It is of the first importance to save all the powder. The cavalry and artillery of the army are still scattered for want of provender and our supply and ammunition trains, which ought to be with the army in case of a sudden movement, are absent collecting provisions and forage. You will see to what straits we are reduced; but I trust to work out."

At last, on March 29th, 1865, Grant pushed forward 50,000 cavalry and infantry to execute the very move which Lee had outlined and for which he was as thoroughly prepared as it was possible to be with the men he had on hand. But to check this advance which threatened to surround his army and cut off his retreat, he had to withdraw the troops guarding the defenses of Petersburg, abandoning some of the intrenchments altogether and leaving nothing much more formidable than a skirmish line anywhere along his front. Even then he could not stop the onrush of the Union troops, which, under Sheridan, circled his right on April 1st and drove back his men in the fierce engagement known as the battle of Five Forks. With the news of this success Grant promptly ordered an assault against the intrenchments and his troops tore through the almost defenseless lines in several places, encountering little or no resistance.

Petersburg was not yet taken, but Lee immediately saw that to protect it further would be to sacrifice his entire army. He, therefore, sent a dispatch to Richmond, advising the immediate evacuation of the city. "I see no prospect of doing more than hold our position here till night. I am not certain that I can do that," he wrote. But he did hold on till the Confederate authorities had made their escape, and then on the night of April 2nd he abandoned the capital which he had successfully defended for four years and started on a hazardous retreat.

The one chance of saving his army lay in reaching the mountains to the west, before Grant could bar the road, but his men were in no condition for swift marching and the provision train which he had ordered to meet him at Amelia Court House failed to put in an appearance, necessitating a halt. Every moment was precious and the delay was exasperating, but he did his best to provide some sort of food for his famished men and again sent them on their way.

By this time, however, the Union troops were hot upon their trail and soon their rear-guard was fighting desperately to hold the pursuit in check. Now and again they shook themselves free, but the moment they paused for food or rest they were overtaken and the running fight went on. Then, little by little, the pursuing columns began to creep past the crumbling rear-guard; cavalry pounced on the foragers searching the countryside for food and captured the lumbering provision-wagons and the railroad supply trains which had been ordered to meet the fleeting army, while hundreds upon hundreds of starving men dropped from the ranks as they neared the bypaths leading to their homes.

Still some thousands held together, many begging piteously for food at every house they passed and growing weaker with each step, but turning again and again with a burst of their old spirit to beat back the advance-guard of the forces that were slowly enfolding them.

"There was as much gallantry displayed by some of the Confederates in these little engagements as was displayed at any time during the war, notwithstanding the sad defeats of the past week," wrote Grant many years later, and it was this splendid courage in the face of hardship and disaster that enabled the remnants of the once invincible army to keep up their exhausting flight. As they neared Appomattox Court House, however, the blue battalions were closing in on them from every side like a pack of hounds in full cry of a long-hunted quarry and escape was practically cut off.

For five days Grant had been in the saddle personally conducting the pursuit with restless energy, and he knew that he was now in a position to strike a crushing blow, but instead of ordering a merciless attack, he sent the following letter to Lee:

"Headquarters Armies of the U.S. "5 P.M. Apr. 7, 1865.

"General R. E. Lee,--Commanding Confederate States Armies.

"The results of the last week must convince you of the hopelessness of further resistance on the part of the Army of Northern Virginia in this struggle. I feel that it is so and regard it as my duty to shift from myself the responsibility of any further effusion of blood by asking of you the surrender of that portion of the Confederate

States Army known as the Army of Northern Virginia.

"U. S. Grant, "Lieut. General.""

Meanwhile the retreating columns staggered along, their pace growing slower and slower with every mile, and at last a courier arrived bearing Lee's reply.

"General:

"I have received your note of this day. Though not entertaining the opinion you express on the hopelessness of further resistance on the part of the Army of Northern Virginia I reciprocate your desire to avoid useless effusion of blood and therefore, before considering your proposition, ask the terms you will offer on condition of its surrender.

"R. E. Lee, "General.""

Grant promptly responded that peace being his great desire, there was only one condition he would insist upon and that was that the surrendered men and officers should not again take up arms against the United States until properly exchanged.

But Lee was not yet ready to yield and continuing to move forward with his faithful veterans, he sent a dignified reply, declining to surrender but suggesting a meeting between himself and Grant, with the idea of seeing if some agreement could not be reached for making peace between the two sections of the country.

This was not the answer that Grant had hoped for, but he had too much admiration for his gallant adversary to ride rough shod over him when he held him completely in his power, and while he gave the necessary orders to prepare for closing in, he sent another courteous note to Lee dated April 9, 1865:

"General.

"Your note of yesterday is received. I have no authority to treat on the subject of peace; the meeting proposed for 10 A.M. today could lead to no good. I will state, however, General, that I am equally anxious for peace with yourself and the whole North entertains the same feeling. The terms upon which peace can be had are well understood.... Seriously hoping that all our difficulties may be settled without the loss of another life, I subscribe myself, etc.,

"U. S. Grant, "Lt. General.""

The courier bearing this message dashed off and disappeared and the chase continued, masses of blue infantry pressing forward under cover of darkness and overlapping the weary columns of gray that stumbled on with lagging steps. Meanwhile, the morning of April 9th dawned and Lee determined to make one more desperate effort at escape. Behind him an overwhelming force was crowding and threatening to crush his rear-guard; on either flank the blue-coated lines were edging closer and closer; but in front there appeared to be only a thin screen of cavalry which might be pierced; and beyond lay the mountains and safety. At this cavalry then he hurled his horsemen with orders to cut their way through and force an opening for the rest of the army, who vigorously supported the attack. It was, indeed, a forlorn hope that was thus entrusted to the faithful squadrons, but they responded with matchless dash and spirit, tearing a wide gap through the opposing cavalry and capturing guns and prisoners. Then they suddenly halted and surveyed the field with dumb despair. Behind the parted screen of horsemen lay a solid wall of blue infantry arrayed in line of battle and hopelessly blocking the road. One glance was enough to show them what Grant's night march had accomplished, and the baffled riders wheeled and reported the situation to their chief.

Lee listened calmly to the news which was not wholly unexpected. There was still a chance that a portion of his force might escape, if he was willing to let them attempt to fight their way out against awful odds, but no thought of permitting such a sacrifice crossed his mind.

"Then there is nothing left for me but to go and see Gen. Grant," he observed to those around him.

But desperate as their plight had been for days, his officers were unprepared for this announcement.

"Oh, General!" one of them protested, "What will history say of the surrender of the army in the field?"

"Yes," he replied. "I know they will say hard things of us; they will not understand how we were overwhelmed by numbers. But that is not the question, Colonel. The question is, is it right to surrender this army? If it is right, then I will take all the responsibility."

No response was offered by the little group and turning to one of his staff, Lee quietly gave an order. A few moments later white flags were fluttering at the head of the halted columns and an officer rode out slowly from the lines bearing a note to Grant.

Chapter XXX
The Surrender

While Lee's messenger was making his way toward the Union lines, Grant was riding rapidly to the front where his forces had foiled the Confederate cavalry. For more than a week he had been constantly in the saddle, moving from one point on his lines to another and begrudging even the time for food and sleep in his efforts to hasten the pursuit. But the tremendous physical and mental strain to which he had subjected himself had already begun to tell upon him, and he had passed the previous night under a surgeon's care endeavoring to put himself in fit condition for the final struggle which Lee's refusal to surrender led him to expect. The dawn of April 9th, however, found him suffering with a raging headache, and well-nigh exhausted after his sleepless night he rode forward feeling more like going to the hospital than taking active command in the field. He had already advanced some distance and was within two or three miles of Appomattox Court House, when an officer overtook him and handed him these lines from Lee:

"Apr. 9, 1865.

"General:

"I received your note of this morning on the picket line whither I had come to meet you and ascertain definitely what terms were embraced in your proposal of yesterday with reference to the surrender of this army. I now ask an interview in accordance with the offer contained in your letter of yesterday for that purpose.

"R. E. Lee, "General."

The moment Grant's eyes rested on these words his headache disappeared, and instantly writing the following reply, he put spurs to his horse and galloped on:

"Apr. 9, 1865.

"Your note of this date is but this moment (11:50 A. M.) received in consequence of my having passed from the Richmond and Lynchburg Road to the Farmville and Lynchburg Road. I am at this writing about four miles west of Walker's Church and will push forward to the front for the purpose of meeting you. Notice sent to me on this road where you wish the interview to take place will meet me.

"U. S. Grant, "Lt. General."

The troops under Sheridan were drawn up in line of battle when Grant arrived on the scene and his officers, highly excited at the favorable opportunity for attacking the Confederates, urged him to allow no cessation of hostilities until the surrender was actually made. But Grant would not listen to anything of this sort, and directing that he be at once conducted to General Lee, followed an orderly who led him toward a comfortable two-story, brick dwelling in Appomattox village owned by a Mr. McLean who had placed it at the disposal of the Confederate commander.

Mounting the broad piazza steps, Grant entered the house, followed by his principal generals and the members of his staff, and was ushered into a room at the left of the hall, where Lee, accompanied by only one officer, awaited him.

As the two commanders shook hands the Union officers passed toward the rear of the room and remained standing apart. Then Lee motioned Grant to a chair placed beside a small marble-topped table, at the same time seating himself near another table close at hand. Neither man exhibited the slightest embarrassment and Grant, recalling that they had served together during the Mexican War, reminded Lee of this fact, saying that he remembered him very distinctly as General Scott's Chief of Staff but did not suppose that an older and superior officer would remember him. But Lee did remember him and in a few minutes he was chatting quietly with his former comrade about the Mexican campaign and old army days.

It would be impossible to imagine a greater contrast than that afforded by the two men as they thus sat conversing. Lee wore a spotless gray uniform, long cavalry boots, spurs and gauntlets, and carried the beautiful sword given to him by Virginia, presenting altogether a most impressive appearance; and his tall, splendidly proportioned figure and grave dignified bearing heightened the effect. His well-trimmed hair and beard were almost snow white, adding distinction to his calm, handsome face without suggesting age, and his clear eyes and complexion and erect carriage were remarkable for a man of fifty-eight. Grant was barely forty-three, and his hair and beard were brown with a touch of gray, but his face was worn and haggard from recent illness, and his thickset figure and drooping shoulders were those of a man well advanced in years. For uniform he wore the blouse of a private, to which the shoulder straps of a lieutenant-general had been stitched; his trousers were tucked into top boots worn without spurs; he carried no sword and from head to foot he was splashed with mud.

He, himself, was conscious of the strange contrast between his appearance and that of his faultlessly attired opponent, for he apologized for his unkempt condition, explaining that he had come straight from active duty in the field, and then as the conversation regarding Mexico continued he grew so pleasantly interested that the object of the meeting almost passed from his mind, and it was Lee who first recalled it to his attention.

He then called for pencil and paper, and without having previously mapped out any phrases in his mind, he began to draft an informal letter to Lee, outlining the terms of surrender. Nothing could have been more clear and simple than the agreement which he drafted, nor could the document have been more free from anything tending to humiliate or offend his adversary. It provided merely for the stacking of guns, the parking of cannon and the proper enrollment of the Confederate troops, all of whom were to remain unmolested as long as they obeyed the laws and did not again take up arms against the Government, and it concluded with the statement that the side arms of the officers were not to be surrendered and that all such officers who owned their own horses should be permitted to retain them.

Lee watched the writing of this letter in silence, and when Grant handed it to him he read it slowly, merely remarking as he returned it that the provision allowing the officers to keep their horses would have a happy effect, but that in the Confederate army the cavalry and artillerymen likewise owned their own horses. That hint was quite sufficient for Grant, who immediately agreed to make the concession apply to all the soldiers, whether officers or privates, observing as he again handed the paper to Lee that his men would probably find their horses useful in the spring ploughing when they returned to their farms. Lee responded that the concession would prove most gratifying to his soldiers, and, turning to his secretary, dictated a short, simple reply to his opponent, accepting his conditions.

While these letters were being copied in ink, Grant introduced his officers to

Lee and strove to make the situation as easy as possible for him. Indeed, throughout the whole interview he displayed the most admirable spirit, tactfully conceding all that his adversary might reasonably have asked, thus saving him from the embarrassment of making any request and generally exhibiting a delicate courtesy and generosity which astonished those who judged him merely by his rough exterior. But Grant, though uncouth in appearance and unpolished in manners, was a gentleman in the best sense of the word, and he rose to the occasion with an ease and grace that left nothing to be desired.

As soon as the letters were signed the Confederate commander shook his late opponent's hand and turned to leave the room. The Union officers followed him to the door as he departed but tactfully refrained from accompanying him further and attended only by his secretary, he passed down the broad steps of the piazza, gravely saluted the group of officers gathered there who respectfully rose at his approach, mounted his old favorite "Traveller" and rode slowly toward his own lines.

By this time the news of the surrender had reached the Union army and cannon began booming a salute in honor of the joyful tidings. But Grant instantly stopped this and ordered that there should be no demonstrations or exultation of any kind which would offend Lee's men. In the same generous spirit he kept his men strictly within their own lines when the Confederates stacked their guns and no one, except the officers assigned to receive the arms, was permitted to witness this final act of surrender[1]. He likewise declined to visit Richmond lest his presence should be regarded as the triumphal entry of a conqueror or smack of exulting over his fallen foes, and with fully a million bayonets behind him ready to win him further glory, his foremost thought was to end the war without the loss of another life. With this idea, on the morning after the surrender, he sought another interview with Lee.

[1]Since the first edition of this volume was published the writer has been furnished, through the courtesy of Mr. Jefferson K. Cole of Massachusetts, with documentary proof that the formal surrender of what remained of Lee's infantry was made in the presence of the First Division of the 5th Corps of the Army of the Potomac, General Joshua L. Chamberlain commanding. Therefore, although it is true that Grant avoided all humiliation of the Confederates, it is evident that a small portion of his troops did witness the final act of surrender, and the statement in the text should be accordingly amended.

Chapter XXXI
Lee's Years of Peace

Desperate as their plight had been for many days, Lee's men had not wholly abandoned the hope of escape, but when their beloved commander returned from the Federal lines they saw by his face that the end had come, and crowding around him, they pressed his hands, even the strongest among them shedding bitter tears. For a time he was unable to respond in words to this touching demonstration, but finally, with a great effort, he mastered his emotion and bravely faced his comrades.

"Men," he said, "we have fought through the war together; I have done my best for you; my heart is too full to say more."

Brief as these words were, all who heard them realized that Lee saw no prospect of continuing the struggle and meant to say so. He was, of course, well aware that the Confederates had many thousand men still in the field, and that by separating into armed bands they could postpone the end for a considerable period. But this to his mind was not war and he had no sympathy with such methods and no belief that they could result in anything but more bloodshed and harsher terms for the South. A word from him would have been quite sufficient to encourage the other commanders to hold out and prolong the cruelly hopeless contest, but he had determined not to utter it.

Grant was firmly convinced that this would be his attitude, but whether he would actually advise the abandonment of the cause was another question, and it was to suggest this course that the Union commander sought him out on the morning after the surrender. This second interview occurred between the lines of the respective armies and as the former adversaries sat conversing on horseback, Grant tactfully introduced the subject of ending the war.

He knew, he told Lee, that no man possessed more influence with the soldiers and the South in general than he did, and that if he felt justified in advising submission his word would doubtless have all the effect of law. But to this suggestion Lee gravely shook his head. He frankly admitted that further resistance was useless, but he was unwilling to pledge himself to give the proposed advice until he had consulted with the Confederate President, and Grant did not urge him, feeling certain that he would do what he thought right. Nor was this confidence misplaced, for though Lee never positively advised a general surrender, his opinions soon came to be known and in a short time all the Confederate forces in the field yielded.

But though peace was thus restored, the war had left two countries where it had found one, and to the minds of many people they could never be united again. It was then that Lee showed his true greatness, for from the moment of his surrender he diligently strove by voice and pen and example to create harmony between the North and South and to help in the rebuilding of the nation. To those who asked his opinion as to whether they should submit to the Federal authorities and take the required oath of allegiance, he unhesitatingly replied, "If you intend to reside in this country and wish to do your part in the restoration of your state and in the government of the country, which I think is the duty of every citizen, I know of no objection to your taking the oath."

He denounced the assassination of Lincoln as a crime to be abhorred by every American, discountenanced the idea of Southerners seeking refuge in foreign lands, scrupulously obeyed every regulation of the military authorities regarding paroled prisoners and exerted all the influence at his command to induce his friends to work with him for the reconciliation of the country. Even when it was proposed to indict and try him for treason he displayed no resentment or bitterness. "I have no wish to avoid any trial that the Government may order. I hope others may go unmolested," was his only comment. But no such persecution was to be permitted, for Grant interfered the moment he heard of it, insisting that his honor and that of the nation forbade that Lee should be disturbed in any way, and his indignant protest straightway brought the authorities to their senses.

In the meanwhile, innumerable propositions reached Lee, offering him great monetary inducements to lend his name and fame to business enterprises of various kinds, but although he had lost all his property and was practically penniless, he would not consent to undertake work that he did not feel competent to perform and would listen to no suggestion of receiving compensation merely for the use of his name. His desire was to identify himself with an institution of learning where he could be of some public service, and at the same time gain the peaceful home life of which he had dreamed for so many years. As soon as this was understood offers came to him from the University of Virginia and the University of the South at Suwannee, Tennessee, but he feared that his association with a State institution like the University of Virginia might create a feeling of hostility against it on the part of the Federal Government, and the Vice-Chancellorship of the Tennessee university would have required him to leave his native state.

Finally, the Trustees of Washington College offered him the Presidency of that institution and the fact that it bore the name of the first President and had been endowed by him straightway appealed to his imagination. At one time the college had been in a flourishing condition but it had suffered severely from the war, much of its property having been destroyed and only a handful of students remained when he was invited to take charge of its tottering fortunes. Indeed, the Trustees themselves were so impoverished that none of them possessed even a decent suit of clothes in which to appear before Lee and submit their proposition. Nevertheless, one of them borrowed a respectable outfit for the occasion and presented the offer with much dignity and effect and Lee, after modestly expressing some doubts as to whether he could "discharge the duties to the satisfaction of the Trustees or to the benefit of the country," accepted the office at a merely nominal salary, closing his formal acceptance of Aug. 11, 1865, with these words: "I think it the duty of every citizen in the present condition of the country to do all in his power to aid in the restoration of peace and harmony and in no way to oppose the policy of the state or general Government directed to that object."

This was the key-note of his thought from this time forward. "Life is indeed gliding away and I have nothing of good to show for mine that is past," he wrote shortly after assuming his new duties. "I pray I may be spared to accomplish something for the benefit of mankind and the honor of God."

It was no easy task to reestablish an institution practically destitute of resources in a poverty-stricken community struggling for a bare subsistence after the ravages of war. But Lee devoted himself body and soul to the work, living in the simplest possible fashion. Indeed, he refused to accept an increase in his meager salary, which would have provided him with some of the ordinary comforts of life, on the ground that the institution needed every penny of its funds for its development. But though the work was hard he took keen pleasure in seeing it grow under his hands, and, little by little, the college regained its prestige, while with the help of his daughters he made his new home a place of beauty, planting flowers about the little house and doing all in his power to make it attractive for his invalid wife.

Thus, for five years he lived far removed from the turmoil of public life, performing a constant public service by exerting a direct personal influence upon the students who came under his charge, and by doing everything in his power to re-unite the nation. Suggestions were constantly made to him to enter politics and had he cared to do so, he could undoubtedly have been elected to the Governorship of Virginia. But he steadily declined to consider this, declaring that it might injure the state to have a man so closely identified with the war at its head and that he could best help in restoring harmony to the country in the capacity of a private citizen.

During all this time he took an active interest in his sons, encouraging them in their efforts to establish themselves and earn their own living, visiting their farms and advising them in the comradely spirit which had always characterized his relations with them. Indeed, every moment he could spare from his collegiate duties was devoted to his family, and his letters to his children, always cheerful and affectionate and sometimes even humorously gay, expressed contentment and unselfishness in every line.

At times it required great self-restraint to avoid bitterness toward the Government, but even when Congress refused his wife's petition for the restoration of the mementos of Washington, taken from her home in Arlington during the war, he refrained from making any public protest and his private comment showed how completely he subordinated his personal wishes to the good of the country.

"In reference to certain articles which were taken from Arlington..." he wrote, "Mrs. Lee is indebted...for the order from the present Administration for their restoration to her. Congress, however, passed a resolution forbidding their return. They were valuable to her as having belonged to her great grandmother (Mrs. General Washington) and having been bequeathed to her by her father. But as the country desires them she must give them up. I hope their presence at the capital will keep in the remembrance of all Americans the principles and virtues of Washington." [These articles were restored to Lee's family by the order of President McKinley in 1903.]

Toward the individuals, however, who had looted his house and appropriated its treasures to their own use, he felt rather differently. But his rebuke to them was written rather more in sorrow than in anger and it likewise reflects the regard for his country which was ever the uppermost thought in his mind.

"...A great many things formerly belonging to General Washington, bequeathed to Mrs. Lee by her father, in the shape of books, furniture, camp equipage, etc., were carried away by individuals and are now scattered over the land," he wrote. "I hope the possessors appreciate them and may imitate the example of their original owners whose conduct must at times be brought to their recollection by these silent monitors. In this way they will accomplish good to the country...."

For his first four years at Washington College Lee accomplished his arduous duties with scarcely a sign of fatigue, but from that time forward his health began to fail and though he kept at his work, it told so heavily upon him that his friends at last persuaded him to take a vacation. He, accordingly, started south with his daughter in March, 1870. Had he permitted it, his journey would have been one continual ovation, for this was the first time he had traveled any considerable distance from his home since the war and people flocked to greet him from all sides with bands and speeches and cart-loads of flowers and fruits. Indeed, it was extremely difficult to escape the public receptions, serenades and other honors thrust upon him, and though he returned to his duties in somewhat better condition, he was soon obliged to retire to Hot Springs, Virginia, for another rest, from which he returned toward the end of the summer vacation apparently restored to health.

Meanwhile he had undertaken various other duties in addition to his collegiate work and some two weeks after the reopening of the college he attended a vestry meeting of the Episcopal Church. At this meeting the subject of rebuilding the church and increasing the rector's salary was under discussion and the session lasted for three hours, at the close of which he volunteered to subscribe from his own meager funds the sum needed to complete the proposed increase of the clergyman's salary. By this time it was seven in the evening and he at once returned to his own house, and finding his family ready for tea, stood at the head of the table as he usually did to say grace. But no words came from his lips, and with an expression of resignation on his face he quietly slipped into his chair and sat there upright as though he had heard an order to which he was endeavoring to respond by remaining at "attention."

Physicians were immediately called who diagnosed the trouble as hardening of the arteries combined with rheumatism of the heart, and though their patient never quite lost consciousness, he gradually fell asleep, and on October 12, 1870, passed quietly away.

Three days later "Traveller," led by two old soldiers and followed by a small but distinguished assemblage, accompanied his master to the grave outside the little chapel which Lee had helped to build for the college which soon thereafter changed its name to Washington and Lee University.

Nothing could have been more grateful to Lee then to have his name thus associated with that of the man whom he revered above all other men and upon whom he had patterned his whole life, and in this graceful tribute he had his heart's desire.

Chapter XXXII
The Head of the Nation

While Lee was passing the closing years of his life in tranquility, Grant was entering upon a stormy career in politics. But before he had any thought of the honors that lay before him he proved himself a good friend to the South and a really great American. Toward his late adversaries he maintained that the true policy was "to make friends of enemies," and by word and deed he earnestly strove to accomplish that result, never losing an opportunity to protect the people of the South from humiliation and injustice. Indeed, if he and some of the other Union commanders had been given complete authority directly after the war, the South would have been spared much suffering and the nation would have escaped some of the evils which inflict it to this day. But Grant's service to the country, as a whole, was far greater than that which he undertook on behalf of any particular section, for at a critical moment he held the destiny of the nation in the hollow of his hand and a word from him would have subjected the people to a military control from which they might never have recovered.

At the time of Lee's surrender the United States had probably the most powerful and the most perfectly equipped army in the world. It was absolutely at Grant's disposal and there were plenty of excuses for employing it in the field, had he been ambitious for military glory. An attack on the French in Mexico or the English in Canada would have been regarded by many people as perfectly justified by their treatment of the United States during the Civil War. But no idea of perpetuating his own power or of making his country a military nation entered Grant's mind. On the contrary, his first thought was to hasten by every possible means the disbanding of the mighty army which hailed him as its chief.

At the close of the war that army numbered over a million men. Six months later only 183,000 remained in the service, and in eight months more the whole force of volunteers had disappeared. No other great commander in the history of the world ever strove thus to deprive himself of power, or with a gigantic instrument of war under his control thought only of peace. Grant was not the greatest military genius of the ages, or even of his own time, but when, with a million bayonets responsive to his nod, he uttered the benediction, "Let us have peace," he took a place apart among those Americans whose fame will never die.

One great triumphant pageant marked the success of the Union cause when the returning armies were reviewed by the President in Washington, cavalry, infantry and artillery by the tens of thousands passing down Pennsylvania Avenue for two whole days, presenting a magnificent spectacle never surpassed in the military annals of any land. But the same spirit which had actuated Grant in refusing to visit Richmond caused him to shun any part of this historic parade, and those who expected to see him on a prancing horse at the head of his veteran troops had little knowledge of his character. He had never made an exhibition of himself at any time during the war, and though he was present on this occasion, he kept in the background and few people caught even a glimpse of him as the well-nigh endless ranks of blue swept by in proud array.

For a time the work of disbanding the army obliged him to remain at Washington, but at the first opportunity he started west to revisit Galena, Georgetown and the scenes of his boyhood days. But, if he hoped to renew his acquaintance with old friends without public recognition and acclaim he was speedily disillusioned, for the whole countryside turned out to welcome him with processions, banners and triumphal arches, hailing as a hero the man who had lived among them almost unnoticed and somewhat despised. Many people had already declared that he would be the next President of the United States, but when some prophecy of this kind had been repeated to him, he had laughingly replied that he did not want any political office, though he would like to be Mayor of Galena long enough to have a sidewalk laid near his home, and this rumor had reached the town. The first sight that greeted his eyes, therefore, as he entered Galena was an arch bearing the words "General, the sidewalk is laid!" and his fellow townsmen straightway carried him off to inspect this improvement, at the same time showing him a new house built and furnished by his neighbors for his use and in which they begged that he would make himself at home.

It was a proud moment for his father and mother when they saw the son who had once disappointed them so deeply received with such marks of affection and honored as the greatest man of his day, and their joy was the most satisfying reward he was ever destined to obtain. But gratifying as all these kindly attentions were the returning hero was somewhat relieved to find that Georgetown, which had largely sympathized with the Confederacy, offered him a less demonstrative welcome. Nevertheless, even there curiosity and admiration combined to rob him of all privacy, and he at last decided to avoid the public gaze by slipping away for one of those long solitary drives which had been his delight in boyhood days. But the residents of the village toward which he turned received word of his coming and started a delegation out to meet him half way. After journeying many miles, however, without seeing any signs of the cavalcade they were expecting, the procession encountered a dusty traveler driving a team in a light road wagon, and halting him asked if he had heard anything of General Grant. "Yes," he reported, "he's on the way," and clicking to his horses quickly disappeared from view. Then someone suggested that perhaps the General might not be traveling on horseback surrounded by his staff and that the dusty traveler who had reported Grant as on the way looked somewhat like the man himself. But the solitary stranger "who looked like Grant" was miles away before this was realized, and when the procession started on his track he was safely out of reach. Doubtless, the sight of this unpretentious man in citizen attire was disappointing to many who expected to see a dashing hero in a gorgeous uniform, but his dislike of all military parade soon came to be widely known. His hosts at one village, however, were not well informed of this, for they urged him to prolong his stay with them in order that he might see and review the local troops which were to assemble in his honor, but he quickly begged to be excused, remarking that he wished he might never see a uniform again.

Certainly there was nothing of the conquering hero or even of the soldier about him when a little later in the course of his duty, he made a tour of the South in order to report on its general condition, and in many places he came and went entirely unnoticed. But though the mass of the people did not know of his presence, he formed an unusually accurate estimate of their views on public questions. "The citizens of the Southern States,…" he reported, "are in earnest in wishing to do what is required by the Government, not humiliating them as citizens, and if such a course was pointed out they would pursue it in good faith." Happy would it have been for the South and for the whole country if this advice had been followed, but the President and Congress were soon engaged in a violent struggle over the reconstruction of the seceded states, and anger, rather than wisdom, ruled the day. In the course of this quarrel Stanton, the Secretary of War, was removed and Grant, temporarily appointed in his place (Aug. 12, 1867), held the office for about five months, thus taking the first step in the long political career which lay before him.

Ten months later he was elected President of the United States and at the end of his term (1872) he was reelected by an overwhelming vote. Those eight years were years of stress and strain, and his judgment in surrounding himself with men unworthy of his confidence made bitter enemies of many of those who had once supported him. He was, however, intensely loyal by nature and having once made a friend he stuck to him through thick and thin, making his cause his own and defending him, even in the face of the facts, against any and all attack. He, accordingly, assumed a heavy burden of blame that did not rightly rest upon his shoulders, but in spite of this many people desired to see him again elected to the presidency and they were sorely disappointed when he refused to become a candidate. On the whole, he had deserved well of the country and the people recognized that he had done much to uphold their honor and dignity, even though he had been too often imposed upon by unreliable and even dangerous friends.

A long tour around the world followed his retirement from the Presidency and his reception in the various countries was a magnificent tribute to his record as a general and a ruler. Meanwhile, an effort was being made by his friends to secure his nomination for a third Presidential term, and shortly after he returned home (1880) he was persuaded to enter the field again. At first he regarded the result with indifference, but as time wore on he warmed with the enthusiasm of his friends and keenly desired to secure the honor. But no man had ever been elected three times to the Presidency and there was a deep-centered prejudice against breaking this tradition. Grant's candidacy therefore encountered bitter opposition, and though a large number of his friends held out for him to the last and almost forced his nomination, General Garfield was finally selected in his place.

This virtually retired him from politics, and to occupy himself and make a living he went into business with one of his sons who had associated himself with certain bankers in Wall Street. Here, however, his notoriously bad judgment of men and his utter ignorance of the business world soon brought him to grief, for he and his son left the management of their firm to the other partners who outrageously imposed upon them for a time and then left them face to face with ruin and disgrace.

The shock of this disaster fairly staggered Grant, but he bravely met the situation and stripping himself of every vestige of his property, including the swords that had been presented him and the gifts bestowed by foreign nations, strove to pay his debts. But, though reduced to penury, he was able to prove his entire innocence of the rascality of his partners and the general verdict of the country acquitted him of any dishonorable act.

To earn sufficient money for his family in their dire necessity he then began to write the story of his military life and campaigns, but in the midst of this employment he was stricken with a most painful disease which incapacitated him for work and left him well-nigh helpless. At this crisis Congress came to his rescue by restoring him to his former rank in the army, with sufficient pay to meet his immediate needs. Then, to the amazement of his physicians, he rallied, and, though still suffering intensely and greatly enfeebled, he at once recommenced work upon his book.

From that time forward his one thought was to live long enough to complete this task, and to it he devoted himself with almost superhuman courage and persistence, in the hope of being able to provide for his wife and family after he had gone. Indeed, in this daily struggle against disease and death he showed, not only all the qualities that had made him invincible in the field, but also the higher qualities of patience and unselfishness with which he had not been fully credited. Uncomplaining and considerate of everyone but himself, he looked death steadily in the face and wrote on day after day while the whole nation, lost in admiration of his dauntless courage, watched at his bedside with tender solicitude.

At last, on July 23, 1885, the pencil slipped from his fingers. But his heroic task was done and no monument which has been or ever will be erected to his memory will serve as will those pages to insure him immortality, for "Grant's Memoirs," modest as the man himself, have become a part of the literature of the world.

Authorities

The following is a partial list of the authorities relied upon in the text:

Grant's Personal Memoirs; Recollections and Letters of General Robert E. Lee (Captain R. E. Lee); Life of Robert E. Lee (Fitzhugh Lee); Robert E. Lee--Memoirs of His Military and Personal History (Long); Military History of U. S. Grant (Badeau); Grant in Peace (Badeau); R. E. Lee--The Southerner (Page); Robert E. Lee (Trent); Robert E. Lee and the Southern Confederacy (White); McClelland's Own Story; Stonewall Jackson and the American Civil War (Henderson); The Story of the Civil War (Ropes); The Rise and Fall of the Confederate Government (Davis); History of the United States (1850-1877 Rhodes); The Campaign of Chancellorsville (Bigelow); Personal Memoirs (Sheridan); Memoirs of General Sherman; Reminiscences of Carl Shurz; From Manassas to Appomattox (Longstreet); Abraham Lincoln--A History (Nicolay and Hay); The Army Under Pope (Ropes); The Antietam and Fredericksburg (Palfrey); The Virginia Campaign of 1864 and 1865 (Humphreys); Chncellorsville (Doubleday); Life and Letters of Robert E. Lee (Jones); Ulysses S. Grant (Wister); Ulysses S. Grant (Garland); Campaigning with Grant (Porter); Autobiography of O. O. Howard.

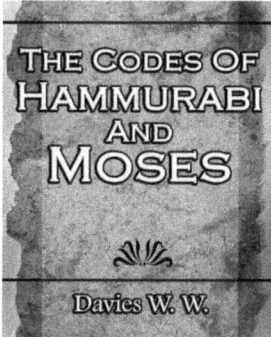

The Codes Of Hammurabi And Moses
W. W. Davies

QTY

The discovery of the Hammurabi Code is one of the greatest achievements of archaeology, and is of paramount interest, not only to the student of the Bible, but also to all those interested in ancient history...

Religion   ISBN: *1-59462-338-4*   **Pages:132**
MSRP $12.95

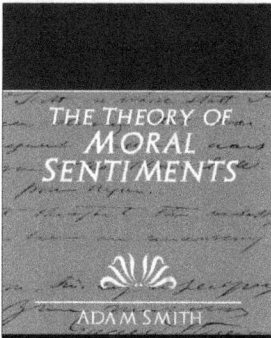

The Theory of Moral Sentiments
Adam Smith

QTY

This work from 1749. contains original theories of conscience amd moral judgment and it is the foundation for systemof morals.

Philosophy ISBN: *1-59462-777-0*   **Pages:536**
MSRP $19.95

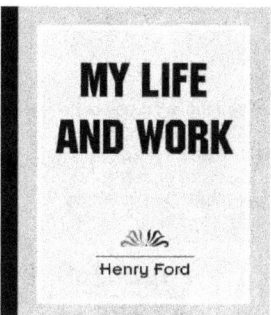

Jessica's First Prayer
Hesba Stretton

QTY

In a screened and secluded corner of one of the many railway-bridges which span the streets of London there could be seen a few years ago, from five o'clock every morning until half past eight, a tidily set-out coffee-stall, consisting of a trestle and board, upon which stood two large tin cans, with a small fire of charcoal burning under each so as to keep the coffee boiling during the early hours of the morning when the work-people were thronging into the city on their way to their daily toil...

Pages:84

Childrens   ISBN: *1-59462-373-2*   *MSRP $9.95*

My Life and Work
Henry Ford

QTY

Henry Ford revolutionized the world with his implementation of mass production for the Model T automobile. Gain valuable business insight into his life and work with his own auto-biography... "We have only started on our development of our country we have not as yet, with all our talk of wonderful progress, done more than scratch the surface. The progress has been wonderful enough but..."

Pages:300

Biographies/   ISBN: *1-59462-198-5*   *MSRP $21.95*

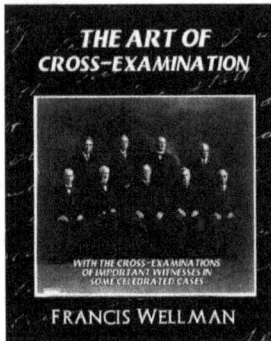

The Art of Cross-Examination
Francis Wellman

QTY

I presume it is the experience of every author, after his first book is published upon an important subject, to be almost overwhelmed with a wealth of ideas and illustrations which could readily have been included in his book, and which to his own mind, at least, seem to make a second edition inevitable. Such certainly was the case with me; and when the first edition had reached its sixth impression in five months, I rejoiced to learn that it seemed to my publishers that the book had met with a sufficiently favorable reception to justify a second and considerably enlarged edition. ..

Pages:412

Reference   ISBN: *1-59462-647-2*   *MSRP $19.95*

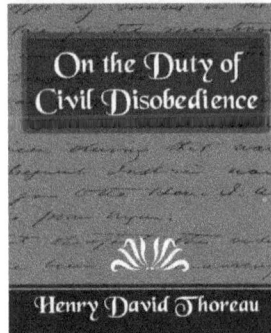

On the Duty of Civil Disobedience
Henry David Thoreau

QTY

Thoreau wrote his famous essay, On the Duty of Civil Disobedience, as a protest against an unjust but popular war and the immoral but popular institution of slave-owning. He did more than write—he declined to pay his taxes, and was hauled off to gaol in consequence. Who can say how much this refusal of his hastened the end of the war and of slavery ?

Law   ISBN: *1-59462-747-9*   **Pages:48**

MSRP $7.45

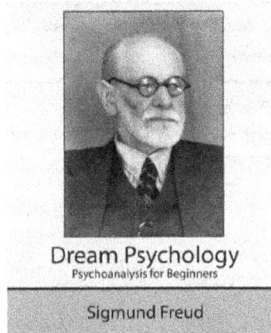

Dream Psychology Psychoanalysis for Beginners
Sigmund Freud

QTY

Sigmund Freud, born Sigismund Schlomo Freud (May 6, 1856 - September 23, 1939), was a Jewish-Austrian neurologist and psychiatrist who co-founded the psychoanalytic school of psychology. Freud is best known for his theories of the unconscious mind, especially involving the mechanism of repression; his redefinition of sexual desire as mobile and directed towards a wide variety of objects; and his therapeutic techniques, especially his understanding of transference in the therapeutic relationship and the presumed value of dreams as sources of insight into unconscious desires.

Pages:196

Psychology   ISBN: *1-59462-905-6*   *MSRP $15.45*

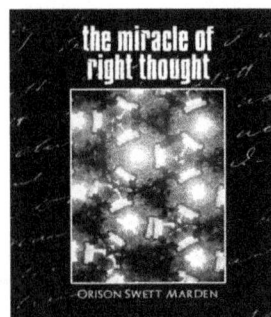

The Miracle of Right Thought
Orison Swett Marden

QTY

Believe with all of your heart that you will do what you were made to do. When the mind has once formed the habit of holding cheerful, happy, prosperous pictures, it will not be easy to form the opposite habit. It does not matter how improbable or how far away this realization may see, or how dark the prospects may be, if we visualize them as best we can, as vividly as possible, hold tenaciously to them and vigorously struggle to attain them, they will gradually become actualized, realized in the life. But a desire, a longing without endeavor, a yearning abandoned or held indifferently will vanish without realization.

Pages:360

Self Help   ISBN: *1-59462-644-8*   *MSRP $25.45*

www.bookjungle.com *email: sales@bookjungle.com fax: 630-214-0564 mail: Book Jungle PO Box 2226 Champaign, IL 61825*

QTY

☐ **The Rosicrucian Cosmo-Conception Mystic Christianity** *by Max Heindel*   ISBN: *1-59462-188-8*   **$38.95**
The Rosicrucian Cosmo-conception is not dogmatic, neither does it appeal to any other authority than the reason of the student. It is; not controversial, but is: sent forth in the, hope that it may help to clear...   New Age/Religion Pages 646

☐ **Abandonment To Divine Providence** *by Jean-Pierre de Caussade*   ISBN: *1-59462-228-0*   **$25.95**
"The Rev. Jean Pierre de Caussade was one of the most remarkable spiritual writers of the Society of Jesus in France in the 18th Century. His death took place at Toulouse in 1751. His works have gone through many editions and have been republished...   Inspirational/Religion Pages 400

☐ **Mental Chemistry** *by Charles Haanel*   ISBN: *1-59462-192-6*   **$23.95**
Mental Chemistry allows the change of material conditions by combining and appropriately utilizing the power of the mind. Much like applied chemistry creates something new and unique out of careful combinations of chemicals the mastery of mental chemistry...   New Age Pages 354

☐ **The Letters of Robert Browning and Elizabeth Barret Barrett 1845-1846 vol II**   ISBN: *1-59462-193-4*   **$35.95**
by Robert Browning and Elizabeth Barrett   Biographies Pages 596

☐ **Gleanings In Genesis (volume I)** *by Arthur W. Pink*   ISBN: *1-59462-130-6*   **$27.45**
Appropriately has Genesis been termed "the seed plot of the Bible" for in it we have, in germ form, almost all of the great doctrines which are afterwards fully developed in the books of Scripture which follow...   Religion/Inspirational Pages 420

☐ **The Master Key** *by L. W. de Laurence*   ISBN: *1-59462-001-6*   **$30.95**
In no branch of human knowledge has there been a more lively increase of the spirit of research during the past few years than in the study of Psychology, Concentration and Mental Discipline. The requests for authentic lessons in Thought Control, Mental Discipline and...   New Age/Business Pages 422

☐ **The Lesser Key Of Solomon Goetia** *by L. W. de Laurence*   ISBN: *1-59462-092-X*   **$9.95**
This translation of the first book of the "Lemegton" which is now for the first time made accessible to students of Talismanic Magic was done, after careful collation and edition, from numerous Ancient Manuscripts in Hebrew, Latin, and French...   New Age/Occult Pages 92

☐ **Rubaiyat Of Omar Khayyam** *by Edward Fitzgerald*   ISBN:*1-59462-332-5*   **$13.95**
Edward Fitzgerald, whom the world has already learned, in spite of his own efforts to remain within the shadow of anonymity, to look upon as one of the rarest poets of the century, was born at Bredfield, in Suffolk, on the 31st of March, 1809. He was the third son of John Purcell...   Music Pages 172

☐ **Ancient Law** *by Henry Maine*   ISBN: *1-59462-128-4*   **$29.95**
The chief object of the following pages is to indicate some of the earliest ideas of mankind, as they are reflected in Ancient Law, and to point out the relation of those ideas to modern thought.   Religion/History Pages 452

☐ **Far-Away Stories** *by William J. Locke*   ISBN: *1-59462-129-2*   **$19.45**
"Good wine needs no bush, but a collection of mixed vintages does. And this book is just such a collection. Some of the stories I do not want to remain buried for ever in the museum files of dead magazine-numbers an author's not unpardonable vanity..."   Fiction Pages 272

☐ **Life of David Crockett** *by David Crockett*   ISBN: *1-59462-250-7*   **$27.45**
"Colonel David Crockett was one of the most remarkable men of the times in which he lived. Born in humble life, but gifted with a strong will, an indomitable courage, and unremitting perseverance...   Biographies/New Age Pages 424

☐ **Lip-Reading** *by Edward Nitchie*   ISBN: *1-59462-206-X*   **$25.95**
Edward B. Nitchie, founder of the New York School for the Hard of Hearing, now the Nitchie School of Lip-Reading, Inc, wrote "LIP-READING Principles and Practice". The development and perfecting of this meritorious work on lip-reading was an undertaking...   How-to Pages 400

☐ **A Handbook of Suggestive Therapeutics, Applied Hypnotism, Psychic Science**   ISBN: *1-59462-214-0*   **$24.95**
by Henry Munro   Health/New Age/Health/Self-help Pages 376

☐ **A Doll's House: and Two Other Plays** *by Henrik Ibsen*   ISBN: *1-59462-112-8*   **$19.95**
Henrik Ibsen created this classic when in revolutionary 1848 Rome. Introducing some striking concepts in playwriting for the realist genre, this play has been studied the world over.   Fiction/Classics/Plays 308

☐ **The Light of Asia** *by sir Edwin Arnold*   ISBN: *1-59462-204-3*   **$13.95**
In this poetic masterpiece, Edwin Arnold describes the life and teachings of Buddha. The man who was to become known as Buddha to the world was born as Prince Gautama of India but he rejected the worldly riches and abandoned the reigns of power when...   Religion/History/Biographies Pages 170

☐ **The Complete Works of Guy de Maupassant** *by Guy de Maupassant*   ISBN: *1-59462-157-8*   **$16.95**
"For days and days, nights and nights, I had dreamed of that first kiss which was to consecrate our engagement, and I knew not on what spot I should put my lips..."   Fiction/Classics Pages 240

☐ **The Art of Cross-Examination** *by Francis L. Wellman*   ISBN: *1-59462-309-0*   **$26.95**
Written by a renowned trial lawyer, Wellman imparts his experience and uses case studies to explain how to use psychology to extract desired information through questioning.   How-to/Science/Reference Pages 408

☐ **Answered or Unanswered?** *by Louisa Vaughan*   ISBN: *1-59462-248-5*   **$10.95**
Miracles of Faith in China   Religion Pages 112

☐ **The Edinburgh Lectures on Mental Science (1909)** *by Thomas*   ISBN: *1-59462-008-3*   **$11.95**
This book contains the substance of a course of lectures recently given by the writer in the Queen Street Hail, Edinburgh. Its purpose is to indicate the Natural Principles governing the relation between Mental Action and Material Conditions...   New Age/Psychology Pages 148

☐ **Ayesha** *by H. Rider Haggard*   ISBN: *1-59462-301-5*   **$24.95**
Verily and indeed it is the unexpected that happens! Probably if there was one person upon the earth from whom the Editor of this, and of a certain previous history, did not expect to hear again...   Classics Pages 380

☐ **Ayala's Angel** *by Anthony Trollope*   ISBN: *1-59462-352-X*   **$29.95**
The two girls were both pretty, but Lucy who was twenty-one who supposed to be simple and comparatively unattractive, whereas Ayala was credited, as her Bombwhat romantic name might show, with poetic charm and a taste for romance. Ayala when her father died was nineteen...   Fiction Pages 484

☐ **The American Commonwealth** *by James Bryce*   ISBN: *1-59462-286-8*   **$34.45**
An interpretation of American democratic political theory. It examines political mechanics and society from the perspective of Scotsman James Bryce   Politics Pages 572

☐ **Stories of the Pilgrims** *by Margaret P. Pumphrey*   ISBN: *1-59462-116-0*   **$17.95**
This book explores pilgrims religious oppression in England as well as their escape to Holland and eventual crossing to America on the Mayflower, and their early days in New England...   History Pages 268

www.**bookjungle**.com *email: sales@bookjungle.com fax: 630-214-0564 mail: Book Jungle PO Box 2226 Champaign, IL 61825*

QTY

The Fasting Cure *by Sinclair Upton*   ISBN: *1-59462-222-1*   **$13.95**
In the Cosmopolitan Magazine for May, 1910, and in the Contemporary Review (London) for April, 1910, I published an article dealing with my experi-
ences in fasting. I have written a great many magazine articles, but never one which attracted so much attention... New Age/Self Help/Health Pages 164

Hebrew Astrology *by Sepharial*   ISBN: *1-59462-308-2*   **$13.45**
In these days of advanced thinking it is a matter of common observation that we have left many of the old landmarks behind and that we are now pressing
forward to greater heights and to a wider horizon than that which represented the mind-content of our progenitors... Astrology Pages 144

Thought Vibration or The Law of Attraction in the Thought World   ISBN: *1-59462-127-6*   **$12.95**

by William Walker Atkinson   Psychology/Religion Pages 144

Optimism *by Helen Keller*   ISBN: *1-59462-108-X*   **$15.95**
Helen Keller was blind, deaf, and mute since 19 months old, yet famously learned how to overcome these handicaps, communicate with the world, and
spread her lectures promoting optimism. An inspiring read for everyone... Biographies/Inspirational Pages 84

Sara Crewe *by Frances Burnett*   ISBN: *1-59462-360-0*   **$9.45**
In the first place, Miss Minchin lived in London. Her home was a large, dull, tall one, in a large, dull square, where all the houses were alike, and all the
sparrows were alike, and where all the door-knockers made the same heavy sound... Childrens/Classic Pages 88

The Autobiography of Benjamin Franklin *by Benjamin Franklin*   ISBN: *1-59462-135-7*   **$24.95**
The Autobiography of Benjamin Franklin has probably been more extensively read than any other American historical work, and no other book of its kind
has had such ups and downs of fortune. Franklin lived for many years in England, where he was agent... Biographies/History Pages 332

Name	
Email	
Telephone	
Address	
City, State ZIP	

☐ **Credit Card**   ☐ **Check / Money Order**

Credit Card Number	
Expiration Date	
Signature	

Please Mail to: Book Jungle
                  PO Box 2226
                  Champaign, IL 61825
or Fax to: 630-214-0564

ORDERING INFORMATION
web: *www.bookjungle.com*
email: *sales@bookjungle.com*
fax: *630-214-0564*
mail: *Book Jungle PO Box 2226 Champaign, IL 61825*
or PayPal *to sales@bookjungle.com*

Please contact us for bulk discounts

DIRECT-ORDER TERMS

**20% Discount if You Order
Two or More Books**
Free Domestic Shipping!
Accepted: Master Card, Visa,
Discover, American Express

www.ingramcontent.com/pod-product-compliance
Lightning Source LLC
Chambersburg PA
CBHW080531090426
42733CB00015B/2555

9 781438 536330